KU-323-452

FLASH REVISE!

HIGHER
ENGLISH

Close Reading

Colin Eckford

HODDER
GIBSON
AN HACHETTE UK COMPANY

Orders: please contact Bookpoint Ltd, 130 Milton Park, Abingdon, Oxon OX14 4SB. Telephone: (44) 01235 827720. Fax: (44) 01235 400454. Lines are open 9.00–5.00, Monday to Saturday, with a 24-hour message answering service. Visit our website at www.hoddereducation.co.uk. Hodder Gibson can be contacted direct on: Tel: 0141 848 1609; Fax: 0141 889 6315; email: hoddergibson@hodder.co.uk

First published in 2012 by
Hodder Gibson, an imprint of Hodder Education,
An Hachette UK Company
2a Christie Street
Paisley PA1 1NB

Impression number   5 4 3 2
Year   2014 2013 2012

Cover photo © javier – Fotolia.com
Typeset in Gill Sans Alternative by GreenGate Publishing Services, Tonbridge, Kent
Printed in Great Britain by CPI (UK) Ltd, Croydon, CR0 4YY

A catalogue record for this title is available from the British Library

ISBN: 978 1444 158694

Contents

1 Understanding 1
2 Understanding 2
3 Understanding 3
4 Understanding 4
5 Understanding 5
6 Understanding 6
7 Understanding 7
8 Understanding 8
9 Understanding 9
10 Linking 1
11 Linking 2
12 Linking 3
13 Summary 1
14 Summary 2
15 Summary 3
16 Summary 4
17 Summary 5
18 Summary 6
19 Summary 7
20 Summary 8
21 Word Choice 1
22 Word Choice 2
23 Word Choice 3
24 Word Choice 4
25 Word Choice 5
26 Word Choice 6
27 Word Choice 7
28 Word Choice 8
29 Word Choice 9
30 Word Choice 10
31 Imagery 1
32 Imagery 2
33 Imagery 3
34 Imagery 4
35 Imagery 5
36 Imagery 6
37 Imagery 7
38 Imagery 8
39 Imagery 9
40 Imagery 10

41 Sentence Structure 1
42 Sentence Structure 2
43 Sentence Structure 3
44 Sentence Structure 4
45 Sentence Structure 5
46 Sentence Structure 6
47 Sentence Structure 7
48 Sentence Structure 8
49 Sentence Structure 9
50 Sentence Structure 10
51 Writer's Language 1
52 Writer's Language 2
53 Writer's Language 3
54 Writer's Language 4
55 Writer's Language 5
56 Writer's Language 6
57 Writer's Language 7
58 Writer's Language 8
59 Writer's Language 9
60 Writer's Language 10
61 Tone 1
62 Tone 2
63 Tone 3
64 Tone 4
65 Tone 5
66 Tone 6
67 Tone 7
68 Tone 8
69 Tone 9
70 Tone 10

Introduction

This book allows you to practise specific aspects of your Higher Close Reading, without having to read entire passages. All the extracts are from sources typical of those chosen for the exam, and all the questions are similar to those which occur every year in the exam.

There is one difference though: in the 'Analysis' questions, I haven't allocated a specific number of marks. However, you should be familiar with how the marks are usually allocated: typically 2 marks for individual questions on Word Choice, Imagery, Sentence Structure or Tone, and 4 marks for 'Writer's use of language'. With this book you can either stick to the usual number of points, or – and this I strongly recommended – you can try aiming for as many as possible. This way you'll get the benefit of the extra practice.

Study all the 'suggested answers' carefully – this should give you helpful ideas for how to word future answers.

I also strongly recommend that you write down your answers – even if it's only scribbles on a scrap of paper – and don't just 'do it in your head'.

Finally, all the articles from which the extracts are taken are available online, so if some of the extracts arouse your interest and you'd like to read the whole article, then just put a key phrase or sentence into a search engine and you should find it right away.

Understanding 1

An extract from an article in the Independent *newspaper, in which Johann Hari writing about the impact of the Internet describes it as being the same as the invention of the printing press over 500 years earlier:*

> It is increasingly clear that the Internet is going to be a transformative moment in human history as significant as the printing press. A decade after Johannes Gutenberg invented it, even the most astute watchers could have only begun to squint at the changes the printing press would spur. In time, it made popular nationalism possible, because linguistic communities could communicate with each other independently, in one language, and form a sense of community. It dissolved the medieval stranglehold of information held by churches and Kings, making it possible for individuals to read the Bible for themselves – and to reject violently the readings used by authority to strengthen its rule. Communications technologies rewire our brains; they make us into a different species.

Q   In what two ways, according to the writer, was the invention of printing 'a transformative moment in human history'?   [2 marks]

ANSWERS ▶▶

1 It increased people's sense of national/racial identity – because it allowed them to share ideas in a common language.

2 It reduced the ability of organised religion and monarchs to control information and/or increased people's freedom to think for themselves/disagree with those who tried to control them – because they could read the Bible for themselves.

***Exam* tip:** Remember that in all Understanding questions you have to use your *own words as far as is reasonably possible* – which means you don't have to put everything into your own words, but you must show you understand the important ideas. For example, here you wouldn't be expected to use alternative words for 'printing' or 'church' or 'Bible', but you couldn't just quote 'dissolved the medieval stranglehold of information'.

Understanding 2

An extract from an article in The Times *newspaper, in which Janice Turner looks at different ways of improving 'public good manners':*

> The consensus on what constitutes public good manners has broken down to the extent that Transport for London is now running a multimillion-pound campaign just to remind us not to eat stinking burgers on the Tube and to give up our bus seats for old folk.
>
> I suppose we should be grateful that, instead of threatening more penalties, they are calling upon our better nature. The Government, on the other hand, seems to live under the delusion that if just one more pleasure is prohibited, another set of draconian rules introduced, 1,000 more speed cameras installed, a CCTV mounted on every corner, human beings will at last fall into line.

Q What, according to the writer, is the fundamental difference in approach between Transport for London and the Government?

[2 marks]

ANSWERS

1 Transport for London are asking/encouraging people to behave in a certain way.

2 The Government is legislating/compelling/threatening punishment if people don't behave in a certain way.

Understanding 3

An extract from an article in the Irish Times *newspaper, in which Fintan O'Toole discusses recent developments in film-making in the USA, particularly an increase in long sequences without dialogue. He starts by describing the 2008 Disney film* Wall-E:

> The film *Wall-E* is over-rated. After the first 20 minutes, the Pixar animation is essentially a standard Disney cartoon. It is technically brilliant, slick and witty, but it follows the well-worn formula of cute anthropomorphic creatures (albeit robots instead of animals) struggling against overwhelming odds, finding love, winning through and delivering the anticipated charge of sentimental uplift.
>
> But those first 20 minutes are really something. It is not just the relative courage of the dystopian vision of an uninhabitable earth or the visual richness of the imagery. It is the fact that a company as mainstream as Disney has returned to wordless story-telling. The fascination of *Wall-E* is that it is stunning up to the point when dialogue is introduced, after which it becomes clever but familiar entertainment.

Q Why does the writer prefer the first 20 minutes of the film to the rest of it? [4 marks]

ANSWERS ▶▶

At least two from each list.

First 20 minutes

- brave/bold idea of showing an earth in which everything is bad
- and which won't support life
- the film is beautiful to look at
- the narrative is told without speech.

Rest of film

- enjoyable and clever
- but it is just a typical Disney cartoon/animation/production
- it follows a standard pattern
- a struggle eventually won by underdogs
- a happy, over-romantic, slushy ending.

Understanding 4

An extract from an article in the Independent *newspaper, in which Amol Rajan argues that too many people are going to University:*

The post-war cult of egalitarianism, with its laudable motive of extending university access to the poor, has driven the rapid expansion of the university sector. Egalitarianism is fundamentally opposed to discrimination of any kind, but discrimination on the basis of ability had been the historic foundation of the university. The two are therefore incompatible: either universities oppose egalitarianism by discriminating on the basis of ability; or they refuse to discriminate, and so stop being universities. Thus we have gone from a system founded on the principle that university is for the brightest, regardless of background, to one in which university is for all, regardless of ability.

This means that, each year, thousands of non-academic students are packed off to do three or four years of ... nothing much. But the exponential growth in university numbers, and with it the redefinition of "degree" to include such notorious absurdities as golf course management, pig enterprise management, and Madonna studies, has produced just such a situation.

Q Why, according to the writer, is it wrong for so many people to go to university? [3 marks]

ANSWERS

Key point

A belief in equality has led to a dislike of making distinctions about people's ability.

Supporting points

1 If universities can't make such distinctions, they have to cater to people of low intelligence.

2 Consequently the idea of a 'degree' has been devalued.

Understanding 5

An extract from an article in the Scotsman *newspaper on 25 March 2011, in which Joyce McMillan writes about Elizabeth Taylor, a famous actress in the 50s and 60s who died that week:*

> Of course, those born since the 1970s may find celebrity on the Taylor scale hard to understand. The whole concept of celebrity has been degraded, over the last two decades, by an avalanche of media coverage which makes no pretence of interest in the actual work that well-known people do, but instead focuses entirely and insidiously on the personal lives, and most particularly the personal appearance, of anyone who has ever been in the public eye for anything, from behaving like an idiot on reality television, to having sex with a Premier League footballer.

Q What three main criticisms does the writer make of the way the media treat celebrities today? [3 marks]

ANSWERS))

Any three from:

- the media are not concerned with what celebrities actually do for a living (i.e. explaining 'no pretence of interest in the actual work' in your own words)
- the media are only interested in what happens in celebrities' private lives (i.e. explaining 'focuses entirely … on the personal lives' in your own words)
- the media take special interest in celebrities' looks (i.e. explaining 'most particularly the personal appearance' in your own words)
- the media's definition of a 'celebrity' is too wide (i.e. explaining 'anyone who has ever been in the public eye for anything' in your own words).

Understanding 6

An extract from an article in the Independent *newspaper, in which Tom Utley describes his reaction to seeing the world-famous painting* Mona Lisa:

When I finally saw the *Mona Lisa*, after my 50 years on this Earth, I found it a terrible disappointment. I don't know quite what I was expecting. I suppose that I was hoping at least for some glimmer of understanding of why this was the most talked-about painting in the world – at best, for a rush of joy at the sheer beauty of this, the real thing.

What I got instead was, well, the *Mona Lisa* – looking exactly as she does on a trillion coffee mugs, posters and tea-towels the world over.

My fellow tourists and I were not really at the Louvre in quest of aesthetic pleasure. We were there just to tick the box marked *"Mona Lisa"*. We traipse around galleries because we know that this is a civilised thing to do. We certainly try to enjoy what we see, and of course some paintings strike us as quite pleasing. But not as pleasing as all that.

Q What is the main point the writer is making about why we visit art galleries? [1 mark]

ANSWERS ▸▸

One from:

- we do it because we think it is the right thing to do
- we do it just so that we can say we've done it.

Understanding 7

An extract from an article in the Sunday Times *newspaper, in which Christopher Goodwin discusses the popularity of the film* The Dark Knight:

> Every decade or so, a film passes from box-office hit to cultural phenomenon. That's what is happening with *The Dark Knight*, the latest instalment in the *Batman* franchise. Even in Hollywood, nobody can quite believe how big a hit the film has become. It has already overtaken the original *Star Wars* to become the second-highest-grossing movie of all time in North America. It might soon pass the $600m made by *Titanic*.
>
> Why has *The Dark Knight*, exceedingly bleak and violent, touched such a cultural nerve? Some believe it was the intense and to some extent morbid interest generated by the untimely death of the co-star, Heath Ledger. Certainly, Warner Bros capitalised on this by featuring his leering, paint-smeared face on almost all the movie's advertising.
>
> That doesn't, however, fully explain why the film has become such an extraordinary cultural phenomenon. Some commentators in America believe the film beguiles audiences with what appears to be popular, comic-book entertainment, but which in fact explores some of the most critical social and ethical issues we face today — in particular, the issues being wrestled with by countries, notably America, fighting the "war on terror". As those who have seen it will know, *The Dark Knight* explicitly examines how far it is permissible for individuals and society to go in the fight against "evil".

 Explain the reasons for the success of *The Dark Knight* offered in:
  a the second paragraph [1 mark] **b** the third paragraph [3 marks]

 ANSWERS ▶▶

a The powerful/strong interest which came about because of Heath Ledger's death.

b **i** Its simple, black-and-white storyline makes it enjoyable/easily accessible …

    ii in addition it probes/looks at/examines important moral issues for society …

    iii in particular the issue of how to face up to or combat forces intent on destroying society.

Understanding 8

An extract from an article in the Independent *newspaper, in which Johann Hari discusses the development of the Internet and of social networking sites:*

> Recently, an old friend I hadn't seen for 10 years committed suicide. I instinctively went to her Facebook page, and so, it seemed, had everyone else who knew her, leaving messages of regret and love and loss. I found myself reading over her old status updates. She was clearly trying to communicate pain and isolation – but we all missed it, leaving inane comments and thumbs up and tossed sheep below every plea for help. Could we have known, if we had read it less casually?
>
> The contrast between the transitory nature of a Facebook status update and the permanence of death made me wonder if all this social networking is actually a way of keeping people at a distance – a way of having a "friend" but not having any of the commitments and duties of friendship, a way to pretend we are together, when in reality we are alone.

Q What key criticisms is the writer making here of Facebook? [3 marks]

ANSWERS >>

1 Most people treat it superficially/don't read the messages carefully enough.

2 It is not about genuine 'friendship'.

3 Far from bringing people together it actually keeps them apart.

Understanding 9

An extract from an article in the Herald *newspaper, in which Ian Bell defends JK Rowling, author of the* Harry Potter *books, against criticism that she is too concerned with money:*

> JK Rowling will never win the Nobel prize for Literature. On any technical level, her writing is not brilliant. But what use is brilliant writing if – the usual result – it isn't read? Fiction isn't supposed to be grand opera. It has only recently pretended to be an art.
>
> Dickens knew all about these things. He offended his betters by making absurd amounts of money. He flogged cheap editions on railway platforms. They called him a hack, and denounced "Dickensian" as a marketing game. He didn't deny a word of it. His only answer was that he was a writer, first and last: his job was to make people read.
>
> Rowling's glory is that she caused an epidemic of childhood reading in a digital world.

Q What, according to the writer, makes JK Rowling and Dickens similar?
[3 marks]

ANSWERS 〉〉

1 Both encouraged widespread reading.
2 Both were very popular with the public.
3 Neither was bothered by criticism.

Linking 1

An extract from an article in USA Today *newspaper, in which Kevin Maney is surprised about some new thinking on the value of video games:*

It's summer vacation. The kids have acres of time to fill. So, of course, they're in the basement playing some video game that involves either weapons or skateboards. Who can doubt that their minds are turning into chipped beef on toast as they sit in the dim light, their educations and social lives leaking away? As a conscientious parent, I feel a gravitational pull to say these words: "Turn that off and read a book!" Or play piano, or run outside, or get in a street fight. Anything but play more video games.

Except apparently that kind of thinking is all wrong. It is about to become as dated as the four basic food groups, the philosophy of spare the rod and spoil the child, and asbestos as a safety feature. Video games might be about the best thing your kids can do to ensure their future success. Better, even, than reading. Which feels a lot like the moment in *Sleeper* when Woody Allen finds out that in 2173, cream pies and hot fudge are health foods.

Q Referring to specific words and phrases, show how the sentence 'Except that … all wrong' acts as a link between the two paragraphs.
[2 marks]

ANSWERS

1 'that kind of thinking' refers to the view that video games are detrimental to children and that almost anything else would be better.

2 'all wrong' introduces the counter-argument that criticism of video games is old-fashioned (which the writer finds hard to believe).

Exam tip: Don't just say that a word or phrase 'links to the previous/following paragraph': be very specific about the point or idea it links to and show that you understand it clearly.

Linking 2

An extract from an article in The Times *newspaper, in which Ben Macintyre explores the argument that museums should return items to their 'home country':*

Six million people visited the British Museum last year, from all over the world, free. They flock to the blockbuster exhibitions; but they also come to explore, to fall into unexpected conversations with distant, ancient, foreign peoples. And that, of course, was exactly what the museum's creators imagined when it was founded by Act of Parliament in 1753: a great cornucopia of different civilisations, an encyclopaedic storehouse of universal knowledge, displaying the great cultures side by side, with equal veneration, to enlighten not just an elite, but the world.

That simple, brilliant idea is now under assault from the concept of "cultural property", a struggle over ownership of the past. In the past half-century, but gathering pace in recent years, so-called "source countries" have successfully begun to reclaim and repatriate artefacts from museums around the world. The governments of Italy, Greece, Egypt, China, Cambodia and other geographical homes of ancient civilisations argue that antiquities in foreign museums are national property, vital components of national identity that should be returned "home" as a matter of moral urgency.

Q Referring to specific words and phrases, show how the sentence 'That simple … of the past' acts as a link between the two paragraphs.
[2 marks]

ANSWERS

1 'That simple brilliant idea' refers to the creators' idea of having a wide range of exhibits from all over the world.

2 'now under assault' introduces the idea that this idea is being attacked by those who believe that all artefacts belong in their country of origin.

Linking 3

An extract from an article in The Times *newspaper, in which Richard Morrison reflects on the number of pubs that are closing, but doubts the claim that it is all the fault of the supermarkets:*

According to the publicans, it's all the fault of the supermarkets, who offer alcohol at astonishingly irresponsible cut-prices and make getting drunk at home (or in the street) so much cheaper than going to a pub that, in these turbulent economic times, there's really no contest for the impoverished serious drinker.

But fashionable though it is to lay the blame for all social ailments at the doors of the giant supermarkets, this particular thesis doesn't quite add up.

After all, supermarkets also flog coffee, yet the invasion of every high street by Starbucks, Costa, Caffè Nero and all those other interchangeable coffee chains suggests that people are quite happy to frequent establishments selling exorbitantly priced beverages if the ambience is congenial and the clientele civilised. The coffee shops appeal to people who would nowadays never dream of spending an hour in the local boozer.

Q Referring to specific words or phrases, show how the second paragraph acts as a link between the other two paragraphs.

[2 marks]

ANSWERS ▶▶

1   'blame' refers to the claim in the first paragraph that supermarkets selling alcohol cheaply is why so many pubs have closed.

2   'doesn't quite add up' introduces the idea that, according to the writer, there is a flaw in their argument, which he exposes in the next paragraph.

Summary 1

An extract from an article in the Sunday Times *newspaper by Tim Wu:*

How hard would it be to go for a week without Google? Or, to up the ante, without Facebook, Twitter and Google? It's not impossible, but even for a moderate Internet user it would be a genuine pain. Forgoing Google is inconvenient; forgoing Facebook or Twitter is to give up whole categories of online activity. When you think about it, it's almost certainly harder to avoid the Internet's dominant firms than to bypass McDonald's or Starbucks and the others that dominate what was once called the real world.

The Internet has long been a model for what the free market is supposed to look like: competition in its purest form. Yet with a few exceptions, the main sectors in most of the world are controlled by one dominant company. Google owns search; Facebook runs social networking; eBay rules auctions; Apple dominates online music; Amazon controls books and retail; and so on.

If the Internet was only yesterday an area of free-wheeling competition, how did things get this way? Could it be – contrary to its reputation – that a free market in the context of the Internet engenders monopoly, not competition?

Q What key point is the writer making about the Internet in these paragraphs? [1 mark]

ANSWERS 〉〉

The Internet used to/is thought to offer users the widest possible choice; however, in many important online activities there is no choice at all/a single company is all-powerful.

***Exam* tip:** Be careful in a Summary question to stick to 'key points' and don't give too much detail. It would be unnecessary, and in fact wrong, to mention in this question details such as Facebook, Apple, Amazon or McDonald's.

.

Summary 2

An extract from an article in The Times *newspaper on 1 July 2009 (during the Wimbledon Tennis Championships), in which Magnus Linklater considers whether Andy Murray should be seen as a 'Scottish or a British champion':*

> There is something frankly adolescent about the need to define sporting heroes, politicians, pop stars or celebrity cooks by their nationality first and their achievements second. Surely by now we have outgrown the mentality that saw the need to report the sinking of the *Titanic* with the headline "Aberdeen man dies in liner tragedy" or to detect a centilitre of Scottish blood in a newly elected American president, thus showing that he owes his achievements less to his grasp of democratic principles than to his fortune in having had a great-uncle from Stornoway.

Q What key point is the writer making in this paragraph about Scottish people?   [1 mark]

ANSWERS ▶▶

(Scots have to accept that) people should be appreciated for what they do, for their accomplishments and not for which country they come from.

Summary 3

An extract from an article in the Scotsman *newspaper, in which Joyce McMillan identifies factors which she feels 'contribute to a real sense of traditional family life in meltdown':*

> The first is the relative ease of divorce, which – particularly for low-income families – removes the ancient pressure on women to put up with bad marriages for the sake of respectability. Unhappy wives are now free to leave with their children, a freedom which some men deeply resent.
>
> The second is the growing mobility of society, and collapse of traditional communities, which often leaves the children of bad or broken marriages without a support-network of neighbours and relatives to cushion the blow.
>
> And the third is the remarkably unreconstructed workplace culture within which British parents still have to function, tolerating chronic loss of status and earnings if they make family life a priority, and often having to work unacceptably long hours if they want to remain in employment at all.

Q Summarise briefly three factors which the writer identifies as possible causes of the breakdown of family life. [3 marks]

ANSWERS ▶▶

1 Because divorce is more readily available than before, women can more easily get out of difficult marriages.

2 The decline in established neighbourhood grouping means people are without others to turn to for help.

3 The rigid demands of employment that eats into family time.

Summary 4

An extract from an article in the Guardian *newspaper, in which Madeleine Bunting discusses complaints that London is a city of too many languages:*

> There is an increasingly anxious debate about London as a place of social fragmentation; a lament that it's a city of so many languages we can no longer find the everyday solidarities of sharing public space. Our politics of migration and integration is still beholden to the myth that multiplicity of languages is a curse – a language test is now imposed on prospective British citizens. There's a media campaign excoriating the cost of the translation services that ensure access to public services for ethnic minorities.
>
> Yet the historical reality is that almost all successful societies have been multilingual, and many are today. Across Africa and Asia, it is routine for people to speak more than one language. Britain's monolingual culture of the past century has been entirely atypical, part of a standardisation and centralisation of culture dominated by the state that obliterated dialects and other languages.
>
> Far from being a curse, multiplicity of language is a blessing, an expression of the huge range of human imaginative capability. It does not confuse, but rather enriches our understanding of human nature.

Q Summarise the three key points the writer is making about more than one language being spoken in a city.   [3 marks]

ANSWERS

1   Some believe it is bad for the city/is a threat to its social cohesion.

2   In fact, multilingualism is a feature of many successful countries/cities.

3   It is a positive feature which enhances our understanding of each other.

Summary 5

An extract from an article in Scotland on Sunday *newspaper on 29 March 2009, in which Dani Garavelli compares two figures who were prominent in the news at the time: Sir Fred Goodwin, former Chief Executive of the failed Royal Bank of Scotland, and Jade Goody, the reality TV star who had just died:*

Fred "The Shred" Goodwin and Jade Goody may have come from very different backgrounds, but they have more in common than the passing similarity of their surnames. Both creatures of the zeitgeist, the Paisley-grammar-schoolboy-turned-banker and the Essex-chav-turned-reality-TV-princess knew how to play a world which turned on greed and fame to their advantage, and made bucketloads of filthy lucre as a result. Focused and ambitious, they seemed untroubled by the distress of those on whose backs they trod as they clambered to the top. Both ruthless; both self-obsessed; both fallible. Yet Jade was mourned as a national treasure and lauded by everyone from the Prime Minster to the Archbishop of Canterbury, while the smashing of windows at Sir Fred's £2m Edinburgh mansion as part of a hate campaign by a group called Bank Bosses Are Criminals was greeted with unconcealed glee.

Q Summarise three key similarities and one key difference the writer points out between these two people.   [4 marks]

ANSWERS ▶▶

Similarities

Any three from:

- they both symbolised the spirit of the age
- they were absolutely determined to succeed
- they accumulated/achieved wealth with no concern for others
- they both had weaknesses.

Difference

Goody is regarded with love/admiration; Goodwin is reviled.

Summary 6

An extract from an article in the Herald *newspaper, in which Iain McWhirter considers the impact of the damage to the nuclear reactor in Japan after the earthquake and tsunami:*

> The cost of cleaning up the mess at Fukushima is going to be immense – early estimates put it at one trillion yen for the reactors alone. Then, there are all the businesses that will have to be compensated for losses. Add in the damage to exports – America has now banned the import of Japanese milk and vegetables – plus the cost of the relocating families whose homes are contaminated and you have another trillion or two. But the biggest bill will come from the rest of the nuclear industry. Japan has 55 nuclear power plants and those that aren't actually closed forthwith will need billions spent on additional safety measures. The long tail of a nuclear accident stretches across decades. Estimates of the cost of the Chernobyl disaster in 1986 vary around £200bn, and the sarcophagus that was built around the still radioactive mass is already needing to be replaced. By comparison, the Gulf of Mexico oil spill is a fleeting event.

Q Summarise the reasons for the 'immense' financial cost of the damage to the Fukushima reactor.   [5 marks]

ANSWERS))

1 Repairing/decontaminating the reactors themselves.

2 Reimbursing/paying out to companies who lost money as a result of the incident.

3 Loss of foreign earnings because people won't buy from Japan.

4 Providing new accommodation for families evacuated from the area.

5 Installing extra safety procedures at many other reactors in Japan.

Summary 7

An extract from an article in The Times *newspaper, in which Richard Morrison doubts the value of being able to capture everything on a camera:*

New technology has made it simple to record on camera almost any trivial event. And it's the work of a mouse-click to distribute those images to all and sundry. Yet just because something is technically possible doesn't automatically make it desirable. I wonder if it is starting to impair the transient joy and spontaneity of daily life. This ubiquitous, almost obligatory obsession with capturing even the most private things in life for posterity is starting to rob us of our ability to savour the moment. And if we don't fully savour the moment as it happens, we may miss its significance, pungency and richness. That makes the process of recalling it later much harder. Paradoxically, our click-click obsession with photographing everything may be sapping, rather than enhancing, our brain's ability to revisit old events with pleasure or nostalgia.

"You had to be there" isn't just a cliché. It's also good advice. We should stop trying to freeze-frame treasurable moments for some tomorrow that may never come, or some absentee audience that probably isn't interested anyway, and just enjoy them as they come and go. God knows, they come and go quickly enough.

Q Summarise the key points in the writer's argument against the practice of capturing everything on camera. **[4 marks]**

ANSWERS ▶▶

1 It has become too easy to pass on unimportant images.
2 Just because it can be done doesn't mean it's a good idea.
3 It is spoiling the way we experience and remember events.
4 Memorable incidents should simply be enjoyed as they happen.

Summary 8

An extract from an article in Psychology Today *magazine, in which Carlin Flora suggests that interest in celebrities has similarities with religion:*

John Lennon infuriated the faithful when he said the Beatles were more popular than Jesus, but he wasn't the first to suggest that celebrity culture was taking the place of religion. With its myths, its rituals (the red carpet walk, the handprints in the concrete on Hollywood Boulevard) and its ability to immortalize, it fills a similar cultural niche. In a secular society our need for ritualized idol worship can be displaced onto stars. Nonreligious people tend to be more interested in celebrity culture. For them, celebrity fills some of the same roles the church fills for believers, like the desire to admire the powerful and the drive to fit into a community of people with shared values.

Much like spiritual guidance, celebrity-watching can be inspiring, or at least help us muster the will to tackle our own problems. Oprah Winfrey suffered through poverty, sexual abuse and racial discrimination to become the wealthiest woman in media. Lance Armstrong survived advanced testicular cancer and went on to win the Tour de France five times.

Q Summarise four key similarities the writer sees between celebrity-watching and religion. [4 marks]

ANSWERS 》

1 Both have established traditions and ceremonies.
2 Both satisfy a need to have someone important/influential to look up to.
3 Both bring people together in a common interest.
4 Both can provide guidelines for the way we live/make us achieve better.

Word Choice 1

An extract from an article in the Sunday Times *newspaper, in which Minette Marrin argues that the BBC is no longer providing 'Public Service Broadcasting':*

Public service broadcasting means a network that produces a range of well-made programmes, particularly in less popular genres, which are financed according to their intrinsic needs and not the size of the audience. Chasing ratings is not what the BBC should be doing. Yet the BBC schedules are stuffed with cheap, populist rubbish, which can hardly be said to be needed since commercial producers make them with even greater enthusiasm and vulgarity. Intoxicated with the popularity of such genres, BBC1 and BBC2 have allowed them to run rampant like some nasty kind of pondlife and crowd out other programmes.

Q Show how the writer's word choice in this paragraph makes clear her disapproval of the type of programme currently on the BBC schedules.

Note: There is no specific mark allocation in this Word Choice section – see paragraph two of the Introduction, page 4.

ANSWERS

Possible answers:

'stuffed'	suggests the schedules are filled to overflowing and it is done in a careless, thoughtless way
'cheap'	suggests not just inexpensive but low quality
'populist'	suggests undiscriminating, appealing to the lowest common denominator
'rubbish'	suggests totally valueless, no better than junk waste
'pondlife'	suggests unpleasant, destructive, parasitical, lowest of the low
'crowd out'	suggests aggressive, bullying, disregard for others.

***Exam* tip:** In the exam you would normally be expected to deal with two or three words at most, but usually there will be, as there are here, several possibilities. Take time to look at a number of possibilities and choose the ones you can deal with most comfortably.

Word Choice 2

An extract from an article in The Times *newspaper, in which Janice Turner reflects on how the younger generation appear unable to live without the latest gadgets:*

> We had a power cut on Tuesday evening. I sat in the dark, oddly relaxed. No e-mail. No telly. Not enough torchlight to read by.
>
> Meanwhile, my younger son thrashed from room to room, between Wii console, computer and TV, fretting that the shows he had Sky-plussed wouldn't record, scrabbling to see how much charge was left in his brother's laptop so that he might, at very least, watch a movie.
>
> When I laughed at his techno-junkie despair he exclaimed in white-hot fury: "It's all right for you. To me it's … it's like living in poverty."

Q Show how the writer's word choice in the second paragraph conveys how much the loss of electricity affected the writer's son.

ANSWERS ▶▶

Possible answers:

'thrashed'	suggests uncontrolled, frenzied, slightly aggressive movement
'fretting'	suggests anxious, nervous state of mind
'scrabbling'	suggests desperate, frantic, near-hysterical
'at very least'	suggests he is prepared to accept/welcome whatever he can.

Word Choice 3

An extract from an article in the Guardian *newspaper, in which Hadley Freeman is very critical of the way some of the media write about eating disorders:*

> When I was a teenager, I spent almost three years straight in psychiatric hospitals being treated for severe anorexia nervosa. Unlike some newspaper columnists, I do not feel compelled to talk about my personal experiences with the mental health profession in every article I write. In fact, I try to avoid talking about them altogether, mainly because I hope that I have something more to offer than my history.
>
> However, the nonsense that has been spouted of late in the media about eating disorders is too ubiquitous and too stupid, even by the low standards of the media's usual coverage of the illness. And while I would never claim that my personal experience makes me an expert on the subject, maybe it gives me a different perspective than, say, a lazy news reporter churning out clichés under a deadline or a columnist in search of easy outrage.

Q Show how the writer's word choice in the second paragraph makes clear her contempt for sections of the media.

ANSWERS 〉〉

Possible answers:

'nonsense'	suggests it is completely false, meaningless
'spouted'	suggests that the stories are pouring out in an uncontrolled way, that the media are like some bore who rambles on and on
'(too) ubiquitous'	suggests they can't be avoided, they overrun the media
'stupid'	unequivocal description of the stories as brainless, almost insultingly so
'lazy'	the reporters make minimal effort, not really concerned about the substance of the story
'churning out'	suggests relentless production of something all the same, in large quantities
'clichés'	suggests the stories are predictable, old, tired, generalised
'easy (outrage)'	the reporters are looking to stir up controversy without making much effort, they are lazy, undemanding.

Word Choice 4

An extract from an article in The Times *newspaper, in which Libby Purves describes a campaign to stop the reintroduction of the sea eagle to Suffolk:*

A new sight puzzles winter ramblers in East Suffolk: a bold hand-lettered sign declaring "Say no to sea eagles here". Baffling, at first: not much point in saying "no" to that flying fortress of the bird world, the white-tailed sea eagle. It wouldn't listen.

That, however, is not what the "no" suggests. It is a cry raised by farmers, landowners and level-headed bird-lovers horrified at a plan hatched by the quango Natural England and the RSPB. They want to spend more than £600,000 to introduce the birds to Suffolk. They claim "vast" popular support – though you could doubt the validity of a sample of 500 people asked some saccharine question about whether they fancy seeing one.

Q How does the writer's word choice in the second paragraph make clear her low opinion of the plan?

ANSWERS ▶▶

Possible answers:

'hatched'	suggests something cooked up, devious, devised by rather smug people
'quango'	invariably used as a term of abuse, suggesting bureaucratic interference
'claim'	suggestion of lack of evidence
"'vast'"	inverted commas imply doubt about the accuracy of the claim
'saccharine'	suggests the question was deliberately soft, unchallenging, 'easy to swallow'
'fancy (seeing one)'	imitates the chummy, encouraging way the question was asked.

Word Choice 5

An extract from an article in the Sunday Herald *newspaper, in which Vicky Allan, having described the failure of the 'five a day fruit and veg' campaign, goes on to criticise a similar new campaign:*

> Last week, it was proposed that parents should be exhorted to adhere to the following five-a-day childcare check-list: read to your kids for 15 minutes; play on the floor with them for 10; talk to them for 10 minutes; praise them regularly; and give them a nutritious diet.
>
> The problem isn't the checklist itself, but the "nudge" principle behind the campaign. This politically trendy word litters the report. Governments are becoming overly fond of nudging, manipulating, beguiling and frog-marching us towards the kinds of personal change they say would lead to better health, reduced crime and other grand objectives.

Q Show how the writer's word choice in the second paragraph shows her disapproval of the campaign.

ANSWERS 〉〉

Possible answers:

'trendy'	suggests something driven by a desire to seem fashionable, usually implies something lacking substance
'litters'	suggests the word is overused in the report, strewn haphazardly through it, as if the authors are fixated on it
'manipulating'	suggests rather devious attempt to control ideas, behaviour
'beguiling'	suggests attempt to mislead by appearing attractive on the surface
'frog-marching'	suggests compulsion, forcing people against their will, authoritarian
'say'	perhaps suggests she doubts the truth of what they claim
'grand (objectives)'	suggests their aims are showy, overblown, extravagant, possibly unattainable.

Word Choice 6

An extract from an article in The Times *newspaper, in which Richard Morrison is critical of too much homework in schools:*

> Homework has a lot to answer for. It doesn't mess up every child. But the mental oppression of leaving school for the day, and then facing hours of slog, alienates many. Piling mountains of homework on children is the surest way to turn education into drudgery.
>
> In the 40 years since I last wore a blazer, the culture of excessive homework has become far worse, denying children the time to discover the infinite richness and possibilities of life. The narrowing of the curriculum over the past 30 years – pushing art, music, sport and drama to the margins – is shocking.

Q Show how the writer's word choice in these paragraphs makes clear his disapproval of homework.

ANSWERS ▶▶

Possible answers:

'oppression'	suggests it is tyrannical, psychologically damaging
'slog'	suggests a laborious, unpleasant, unrewarding task
'piling'	suggests an endless accumulation, work stacking up
'mountains'	suggests enormous, daunting amount, something to be climbed with difficulty
'drudgery'	suggests dull, repetitive, tedious, unrewarding chores
'culture'	(in this context) can suggest a misguided belief in something, where people accept something without thinking about it
'denying'	suggests young people are being prevented, kept away from something
'narrowing'	suggests reduction, weakening, lack of breadth, lack of attention to more important matters
'shocking'	suggests he finds it genuinely deplorable, disturbing, upsetting.

Word Choice 7

An extract from an article in The Times *newspaper, in which Alice Miles is critical of the RSPCA:*

> Research by the RSPCA has found that a quarter of schools own pets, ranging from a hermit crab to a horse. Hurrah! A small piece of chaos, of life, amid the regimented drilling that we call school.
>
> But not for much longer, for the RSPCA believes there is a danger that the kids might be too noisy, or the lighting conditions could be wrong, and that the classroom pet may receive variable care from different families at evenings or weekends.
>
> If the RSPCA has its way, no more generations of kids will be taught to care for the school guinea pig or rabbit, or hermit crab; no more learning responsibility and respect for animals, no feeling the joy of holding a live thing in their hands. Laughably, the charity suggests that schools should get a soft toy instead to teach children about animal welfare.

Q Show how the writer's word choice emphasises the positive side of having pets in schools.

ANSWERS ▶▶

Possible answers:

'Hurrah!'	suggests she is cheering in approval
'chaos'	suggests the unpredictable, real-life experience she approves of (as opposed to the 'regimented drilling')
'life'	emphasises the vitality, the excitement offered by contact with animals
'responsibility'	suggests the idea that children's attitudes to others will improve
'respect'	suggests the idea that children will behave better to others
'joy'	emphasises the pleasure, delight, magic of the experience.

***Exam* tip:** This question is about 'the positive side of having pets in schools', so you have to pick words which allow you to comment in relation to that. Words such as 'regimented', 'drilling', 'danger', 'laughably' are all easy to comment on, but are not relevant to this question.

Word choice 8

An extract from an article in the Guardian *newspaper, in which Amelia Gentleman describes the queues in the Louvre in Paris to see the famous painting,* Mona Lisa*:*

> Waiting to see the *Mona Lisa* has all the thrill of standing in an airport check-in queue. The crowd pushes forward, cattle-like and unquestioning, performing a ritual they know they have to go through with in order to complete a pre-ordained tourist experience.
>
> By midday the room is seething with visitors, the line heaves towards the front, a slow, weary museum trudge, and around 70 more people file in every minute. Caged in a box of bullet-proof glass, the picture looks unimpressive under the harsh institutional lighting.

Q Show how the writer's word choice in these paragraphs conveys the unpleasantness of the experience.

ANSWERS ▶▶

Possible answers:

'airport check-in queue'	suggests slow, boring, something that has to be endured, something over which you have no control
'cattle-like'	suggests non-human behaviour, moving together as in a herd, stripped of individuality, heavy/lumbering movement
'ritual'	suggests something very formal, something that must be carried out as instructed, something to be endured
'pre-ordained'	suggests lack of freedom to choose, fixed rules laid down by someone else
'seething'	suggests barely tolerable numbers of people, crammed/stuffed into one space, swirling, out of control
'heaves'	suggests powerful unstoppable movement, crowd of people lurching, lumbering
'trudge'	suggests slow, heavy, lumbering movement, lacking in any pleasure/enjoyment, something done unwillingly/under duress
'caged'	suggests the painting is being kept away from the public, as if it is dangerous, generally sounds unwelcoming
'harsh'/'institutional'	suggests lighting is intrusive, unpleasant, not conducive to an uplifting experience.

Word Choice 9

An extract from an article in The Times *newspaper, in which Simon Jenkins describes the impact of a lively Youth Orchestra playing a 'Prom' concert in London's Albert Hall:*

> London's classical music scene has been in a state of upheaval since the charismatic 26-year-old Venezuelan, Gustavo Dudamel, brought his Simón Bolívar Youth Orchestra to last summer's Proms and tore up the rulebook. After performing a Shostakovich symphony, his sedate rows of dark-suited players suddenly stood up, reversed their jackets to reveal flags, twirled and hurled instruments into the air and swayed into a mambo rhythm. The Albert Hall went berserk.
>
> A lifetime of inhibition imposed by the decorum of the classical repertoire was cast aside in a flash by players and audience alike. The seated musicians, the white tie and tails, the silence and discreet applause, were overnight a century out of date. The concert became a shared experience of raucous laughing and dancing. So much for the prediction that the birth of recording spelled the death of the concert hall.

Q Show how the writer's word choice makes clear the contrast between the kind of orchestral concert people would expect and the one he is describing.

ANSWERS ▶▶

Expected

Possible answers:

'sedate'	suggests calm, rather dull
'inhibition'	suggests repressed, fearful, unadventurous
'decorum'	suggests rather stuffy, formal behaviour
'silence'	suggests almost funereal atmosphere
'discreet (applause)'	suggests quiet, undemonstrative, restrained.

Simón Bolivar Youth Orchestra

Possible answers:

'twirled and hurled'	suggests lively, animated movements
'mambo (rhythm)'	suggests exotic, Latin American, dance-based
'berserk'	suggests audience's wild, unrestrained response
'cast aside'	suggests sudden and total rejection
'raucous'	suggests unrefined, unrestrained, genuine.

Word Choice 10

An extract from an article in the Irish Times *newspaper, in which Fintan O'Toole discusses recent developments in film-making in the USA, particularly an increase in long sequences without dialogue. He starts by describing the 2008 Disney film* Wall-E:

> The film *Wall-E* is over-rated. After the first 20 minutes, the Pixar animation is essentially a standard Disney cartoon. It is technically brilliant, slick and witty, but it follows the well-worn formula of cute anthropomorphic creatures (albeit robots instead of animals) struggling against overwhelming odds, finding love, winning through and delivering the anticipated charge of sentimental uplift.
>
> But those first 20 minutes are really something. It is not just the relative courage of the dystopian vision of an uninhabitable earth or the visual richness of the imagery. It is the fact that a company as mainstream as Disney has returned to wordless story-telling. The fascination of *Wall-E* is that it is stunning up to the point when dialogue is introduced, after which it becomes clever but familiar entertainment.

Q Show how the writer's word choice makes clear his preference for the first 20 minutes of the film over the rest of it.

ANSWERS

First 20 minutes

Possible answers:

'really something'	suggests it is out of the ordinary, has a 'wow' factor
'courage'	suggests that the subject matter is difficult and/or disturbing, but that the film makers are to be admired for tackling it
'richness'	suggests sumptuous, lavish, something really beautiful (Note, not really about rich as in wealthy)
'stunning'	suggests it is breathtakingly, outstandingly good, striking in its qualities.

Rest of the film

Possible answers:

'standard'	suggests nothing special, run of the mill, just another of the same
'(well-worn) formula'	suggests it is done to a pattern, unimaginative, no need to add anything new or exciting
'anticipated'	suggests it is predictable
'sentimental'	suggests it is maudlin, slushy, a bit corny
'familiar'	suggests it is well-known, not challenging, safe.

Imagery 1

An extract from an article in the Guardian *newspaper in March 2011, in which Tony McNulty writes about the importance of the Census:*

> It's time for the 2011 census and I would urge everyone to fill the forms in as best they can and understand that this is a really important exercise. The census is all about providing the state with key demographic data so that it can understand the nature of our communities much better than it does. It is a snapshot of the UK on one particular day in one particular year – but the data gathered has profound ramifications for all communities and for some time to come.

Q Show how the writer's use of imagery clarifies what he is saying about the census.

Note: There is no specific mark allocation in this Imagery section – see paragraph two of the Introduction, page 4.

ANSWERS ▶▶

| 'snapshot' | just as a snapshot captures a picture (of people/places at a certain moment) which can be looked at/studied as often as you like in the future, so the census provides a description of what the country was like on one day. |

***Exam* tip:** Remember that when you're answering an Imagery question, you must give the literal meaning of the word (the 'root' of the image) and then go on to show how the writer is using this idea to explain what (s)he is saying.

Imagery 2

An extract from an article in the Scotsman *newspaper, in which Joyce McMillan argues against those who blame all society's ills on youth crime:*

> Britain, at the moment, is a nation full of respectable citizens –
> people who have played by the rules all their lives – who are waking
> up at night in a sweat of fear over whether they will be able to pay
> the bills, keep up with the mortgage, and even hang on to their jobs,
> as recession bites; and it is understandable that they feel frightened,
> betrayed and angry. It is, though, neither pleasant nor smart of them
> to take the tabloid bait which suggests they should focus that anger
> on a small minority of street-kids who break the rules, rather than
> on those actually responsible for the current state of the global
> economy.

Q Show how the writer's imagery makes clear how 'respectable
citizens' are reacting to youth crime.

ANSWERS ▶▶

Possible answers:

'a sweat of fear'	their fear is like the result of a nightmare which has caused them to panic and wake up bathed in sweat, as if youth crime was invading their rest – suggests youth crime is psychologically disturbing
'bait'	just as bait is designed to lure fish/animals so that they can be captured, so the tabloid press offers its readers the simplistic solution that youth crime is the source of all their problems and thus traps them into a wrong belief.

***Exam* tip:** Remember to stick to the 'focus' in the question – in this case about 'reaction to youth crime'. There are two other images in the paragraph ('played by the rules' and 'bites') but neither would be relevant.

Imagery 3

An extract from an article in the Herald *newspaper, in which Iain McWhirter has been describing the long term effects of damage to a nuclear reactor:*

> The cost of cleaning up the mess at Fukushima is going to be immense. The long tail of a nuclear accident stretches across decades. Estimates of the cost of the Chernobyl disaster in 1986 vary around £200bn, and the sarcophagus that was built around the still radioactive mass is already needing to be replaced. By comparison, the Gulf of Mexico oil spill is a fleeting event.

Q Show how the writer's imagery contributes to his description of the severity of a nuclear accident.

ANSWERS ▶▶

Possible answers:

'long tail'	just as the tail on some animals can be a lengthy extension of the animal itself (or the tail of a comet extends significantly after the comet itself), a nuclear accident has many effects long after the event itself
'sarcophagus'	comparing the concrete encasing of Chernobyl to a massive (ancient) burial tomb emphasises the idea of the death and something enormous which is designed to last for a long time.

Imagery 4

An extract from an article in the Scotsman *newspaper on 25 March 2011, in which Joyce McMillan writes about the actress Elizabeth Taylor, who died that week. McMillan describes just how big a star Taylor was in the 50s and 60s, famous not just for her talent as an actress but for her looks and stormy personal life.*

Of course, those born since the 1970s may find celebrity on the Taylor scale hard to understand. The whole concept of celebrity has been degraded, over the last two decades, by an avalanche of media coverage which makes no pretence of interest in the actual work that well-known people do, but instead focuses entirely and insidiously on the personal lives, and most particularly the personal appearance, of anyone who has ever been in the public eye for anything, from behaving like an idiot on reality television, to having sex with a Premier League footballer.

Q Show how the writer's use of imagery clarifies what she is saying about media coverage of celebrity over the last two decades.

ANSWERS

Possible answers:

'avalanche'	just as an avalanche is a huge amount of snow rushing downhill destroying everything in its path, so media coverage in recent years has grown to such an extent that it submerges everything else
'degraded'	just as a degraded substance has been converted into a substance with a simpler structure, so the media coverage of famous people is now of distinctly lesser quality.

Imagery 5

An extract from an article in The Economist *weekly newspaper, in which the writer traces the way cities have evolved:*

> Throughout history, cities open to the world have benefited both from an exchange of goods and from a trade in ideas from abroad. Japan, by closing its doors to foreigners, condemned its cities to slow marination in their own culture until the country's opening up after 1853. Today the burgeoning cities with the best chance of overcoming their difficulties are those in Asia and Latin America that welcome investment, trade and entrepreneurial fizz from foreigners.

Q Show how the writer's imagery helps to reinforce the contrast between 'open' and 'closed' cities.

ANSWERS ▸▸

Closed cities

'marination'   just as marination involves soaking foods in liquid, often for a long time, before cooking, so Japan, by excluding foreign influences, was immersed in its own culture.

Open cities

'fizz'   just as fizz is the lively effect of bubbles in a liquid, so the influence of foreign businessmen in a city is invigorating.

Exam tip: Because this question asks you about a contrast, you must deal with (at least) two images.

Imagery 6

An extract from an article in the Independent *newspaper, in which Johann Hari argues that people should not be working such long hours:*

> Britain now has the longest work hours in the developed world after the US – and in a recession, those of us with jobs scamper ever faster in our hamster-wheels. Yet the economists and thinkers of, say, the 1930s, assumed that once we had achieved abundance – once humans had all the food and clothes and heat and toys we could use – we would relax and work less. They thought that by now work would barely cover three days as we headed *en masse* for the beach and the concert-hall.
>
> Instead, the treadmill is whirling ever-faster. We don't stop primarily because we are locked in an arms race with our colleagues. If we relax and become more human, we fall behind the person in the next booth down, who is chasing faster. Work can be one of the richest and most rewarding experiences, but not like this.

Q Show how the writer's imagery makes clear his disapproval of current working practices.

ANSWERS ▶▶

Possible answers:

'hamster-wheels'	just as a hamster-wheel is designed for endless repetitive movement and gets the hamster nowhere, so our working lives are tedious and unproductive
'treadmill'	just as a treadmill requires constant effort and is dull and repetitive, so our working lives are dreary and monotonous
'arms race'	just as an arms race involves two sides endlessly striving for ever better weaponry, so our working lives have become over-competitive (to the point where neither 'side' can ever win).

***Exam* tip:** The reference to 'the beach and the concert hall' might be seen as imagery, in that each is symbolic, i.e. 'beach' represents leisure and 'concert-hall' represents cultural pursuits. An answer along these lines would certainly score marks, but the images above are 'safer'.

Imagery 7

An extract from an article in The Times *newspaper, in which Ben Macintyre admits to being overwhelmed by choice:*

> Last week, on holiday in the US, I went to a supermarket near Fort Myers to buy breakfast cereal with the children, and suffered the first of a series of choice overdoses. A vast canyon of cereals stretched to the horizon, a universe of flakes, crunchies, puffs and additives, an overflowing cornucopia of baffling breakfast options. The children whooped, and began grabbing at the boxes. A fight broke out over Trix, Froot Loops, Chex, or Cheerios, and then another over the specific variety of Cheerios.
>
> There are, I subsequently learnt, 275 different sorts of cereal available in the US.

Q Show how the writer's use of imagery adds impact to what he is saying about choice.

ANSWERS

Possible answers:

'overdoses'	just as an overdose is the near-fatal result of having too much of a narcotic, so he feels the amount of choice he faced was damaging to him psychologically
'canyon'	a canyon is a huge gorge or valley which towers over you if you are at the bottom of it; the writer feels that the shelves of cereal were similarly large and intimidating
'horizon'	just as the horizon is the furthest point the human eye can see, so the writer is suggesting the rows of cereals stretched for miles and miles
'universe'	the writer is exaggeratedly suggesting that the huge number of cereal varieties was as large as the known universe – the largest space imaginable
'cornucopia'	just as in painting, sculpture, etc. a cornucopia is a horn full to overflowing with fruit and other produce, so the shop had an excessive abundance of the cereals.

Imagery 8

An extract from an article in The Times *newspaper, in which James Harkin discusses the usefulness of Twitter in reporting worldwide events:*

Twitter is the latest social networking craze to have conquered the ageing mainstream media, and using it is like sending out a universal text message to the whole planet. For many, this orgy of technology-enhanced wittering is simply something that we indulge in during our spare time, but it's not without its uses. Its coming of age is generally dated to the Mumbai terror attacks at the end of November, when minute-by-minute updates of the unfolding chaos zipped around the world from eye-witnesses armed with Twitter on their laptops and mobile phones. It was given another fillip on the geopolitical stage in January, when the Israeli Government used Twitter to snipe at the mainstream media and get across its reasons for invading Gaza.

Q Show how the writer uses imagery in this paragraph to support the points he is making about Twitter in general and the media in general.

ANSWERS ▶▶

Possible answers:

'conquered'	just as to conquer means to fight and then overcome, so the mainstream media have been unable to fight off or resist Twitter, which is now a part of it
'mainstream'	just as the mainstream is the principal current of a river, so the 'mainstream media' refers to the traditional, safe, well-established media
'orgy'	just as an orgy is a wild party involving indiscriminate (sexual) activity, so Twitter is seen by some as an uncontrolled/uncontrollable mess of communication lacking order and decency
'fillip'	just as a fillip is literally a snap of the fingers which suggests quick and lively action, so Twitter was given a snappy boost by the events in the Middle East
'(geopolitical) stage'	just as a stage is where the action of a play takes places, so world events can be seen as being performed, to be watched by the public
'snipe'	just as to snipe is to shoot single targets from a hidden position, so the Israeli Government, instead of launching a full scale attack on the press, made frequent small criticisms.

***Exam* tip:** The six examples above are the easiest examples of imagery to deal with in the paragraph. There are other possibilities ('like sending a universal text message …', 'zipped', 'armed'), but these would not be easy to explain. Key advice: always choose the image(s) you will find easiest to explain.

Imagery 9

An extract from an article in the Observer *newspaper, in which Colin Blakemore (writing about the centenary of the birth of Charles Darwin) considers the way organised religion responds to scientific discoveries which are at odds with church teachings:*

Science has rampaged over the landscape of religious explanation. Church leaders have reluctantly accommodated the discoveries of scientists – with the odd burning at the stake and excommunication along the way. But I was astounded to discover how resistant many Christians are to scientific ideas that challenge Biblical accounts. More than half of Americans, even a third of Brits, still believe that God created humans in their present form. The process of Christian accommodation of science is a bit like the fate of fieldmice confronted by a combine harvester, continuously retreating into the shrinking patch of uncut wheat.

Q Show how the writer's use of extended imagery clarifies his attitude to both science and the Church.

ANSWERS ▶▶

Possible answers:

'Science has rampaged over the landscape of religious explanation'	compares science to a marauding crowd which is destroying everything in front of it; compares religious explanations to scenery in front of us on which the explanations are laid out for us to see – suggests that science is an unstoppable force which has been destroying what religion taught us in the past
'fieldmice … combine harvester … shrinking patch of uncut wheat'	compares believers to small, timid animals; compares science to a large machine which threatens the fieldmice's habitat; compares the areas of religion still unscathed to an increasingly small part of a harvested field – suggests religious arguments are weak and easily confounded and that science is a sophisticated operation which is slowly but unstoppably driving the believers out to the extent that they have little or no argument left.

Exam tip: Extended metaphors such as the two here are often best dealt with not by the 'Just as … so …' approach but by the one shown above which identifies the key comparisons and then explains what is being suggested overall.

Imagery 10

An extract from an article in The Times *newspaper, in which Richard Morrison says he has nothing against new technology, apart from one thing:*

> What I do regret, however, is the built-in obsolescence of so many household items. My parents bought a wooden wireless in 1947, the year they were married. In 1973, the year I went to university, it was still in good health. It sat in the kitchen like an old friend – which, in a way, it was. When my mum replaced it with a newfangled radio that could also play cassette-tapes (gosh, remember them?) I felt a real sense of loss.
>
> I can't imagine ever forming the same sort of intense relationship with a BlackBerry or iPod, for all their flirty party-tricks. How could I? Such is the frenetic turnover of 21st-century technology that there's no time to forge emotional bonds. Owning a gadget these days is more like a one-night stand than a marriage.

Q Show how the writer's extended imagery clarifies his views on the difference between old and new technology.

ANSWERS 》

The extended image compares technology with aspects of human relationships:

- the radio is an 'old friend', suggesting it was something trusted and accepted – a warm, pleasant relationship
- the BlackBerry and iPod have 'flirty party-tricks', suggesting they are superficially appealing, slightly seductive, but insubstantial
- owning a gadget today is like a 'one-night stand', suggesting that, like a brief affair, it might bring momentary pleasure, is over quickly, lacks commitment – unlike 'marriage', which is expected to last a while and give fulfilment.

Overall, the rather light-hearted imagery clearly shows his preference for older technology that lasts, unlike modern technology which quickly loses its appeal.

Sentence Structure 1

An extract from an article in the Scotsman *newspaper, in which Gillian Bowditch examines Scottish attitudes to alcohol:*

What surprises me most is just how much we are deceiving ourselves. For previous generations, alcohol was the most toxic substance around and they treated it with caution and respect. Our society's increased affluence and the supermarkets' role in demystifying wine, have lulled us into believing that alcohol is a wholly benevolent product. We are on the brink of conning ourselves that drinking very high quantities of alcohol on a very regular basis is not only normal but an essential part of staying young and sexy.

The normalisation of excessive drinking is everywhere. Look at something as anodyne as messages on greeting cards. Look at the effect Ibiza culture is having back home. Look at the rise of the superpub. Look at the number of new alcoholic products coming on to the market. Look at the space and prominence supermarkets give to alcohol. Look at television.

We won't change the culture overnight, but we could start to change direction. It's not just about drinking less; it's about thinking more.

Q Show how the writer's sentence structure in the second and third paragraphs emphasises the points she is making.

Note: There is no specific mark allocation in this Sentence Structure section – see paragraph two of the Introduction, page 4.

ANSWERS

Possible answers:

short simple sentence to open paragraph 2	unambiguous statement of the situation acts as a clear introduction to the 'evidence to follow'
repeated use of 'Look at …'	suggests widespread availability of evidence, the problem is everywhere, almost overwhelming
(repeated) use of imperative	suggests writer is urging reader to wake up, pay attention
repetition/balance in 'change … change'	draws attention to the concession 'We won't … but we could'
semicolon in last paragraph	balances the two ideas, emphasising there's more to it than just reducing consumption
'drinking less … thinking more'	parallel structure (and use of rhyme and rhythm) provides a final flourish, again emphasising there are two things to be done.

Exam tip: When you're answering a Sentence Structure question, you have to identify the feature (for example, parenthesis, list, parallelism, punctuation marks) but you don't get any marks for this alone. The marks will come from how well you explain the effect the feature creates in the sentence or paragraph in which it appears.

Sentence Structure 2

An extract from an article in the Herald *newspaper, in which Melanie Reid describes a police operation in the West of Scotland that seized large quantities of drugs and arrested many dealers. She goes on to explain that new dealers will appear within hours, often with contaminated drugs:*

Conventionally, after a huge police effort like this, the response is to sit back in one's armchair happy in the knowledge that the streets have been cleared of an evil scourge that ruins lives. Good has triumphed over evil. Credits roll.

Except that real life doesn't always work that way. Drug raids, to put it bluntly, don't tend to work in reality. They look good on telly. They help senior police officers reach targets. They reassure the public. They may stop a few clubbers enjoying ecstasy this coming weekend. There the benefits end. Unless there is a massive input of drug rehabilitation resources to coincide with the raids (and there almost never is). Without that, these police operations leave communities ultimately worse off, with more crime, more misery and more death.

Q Show how the writer's sentence structure in both paragraphs adds impact to the points she is making.

ANSWERS ▶▶

Possible answers:

positioning of 'Conventionally'	prominently placed at the very beginning to remind us that she is going to describe the 'usual' response – and implying strongly that she is going to show the inaccuracy of this
'Good has triumphed over evil. Credits roll.'	simple sentences implying the simplicity of the thinking; making it sound like a film (fiction)
'They look … They help … They reassure … They may stop'	listing structure to point out all the (superficially) good things the raids achieve, as if building up to the truth of what really happens
'There the benefits end.'	short, abrupt sentence interrupts the flow of all the 'benefits', points out bluntly that these 'benefits' are minimal
'(and there almost never is)'	parenthetical reinforcement of how rarely anything worthwhile follows from raids
repetition of 'more'	emphasises the bleakness of the situation after raids.

Sentence Structure 3

An extract from an article in the Herald *newspaper in March 2011, in which Ron Ferguson describes his reaction when things went wrong with the 21-foot high digital clock in Trafalgar Square to mark the 500th day before the 2012 Games:*

I must admit I laughed aloud when I heard that the digital clock which had been counting down to the Olympics had stopped. Four British Olympic champions started the clock, amidst fireworks and popping of corks; within 24 hours, the display was stuck at 500 days and 7:06:56.

But why laugh because a clock stopped?

It's something to do with ambivalent feelings about modern technology. I enjoy the good things that technology brings, but fear its pervasive, beguiling power. Its innovative drive seems almost miraculous as it delivers benefits, but its liberating tendencies often turn into forms of domination.

Q
  a Show how the sentence structure in the first paragraph draws attention to the stopping of the clock.
  b Show how the sentence structure in the third paragraph develops the idea of the word 'ambivalent' in the first sentence.

ANSWERS ▶▶

a

semicolon in the second sentence	creates balance/contrast between 'started' and 'stuck'
	and/or
	creates balance/contrast between the excitement ('fireworks … popping of corks') of the launch and the way the clock became 'stuck'.

Exam tip: Remember: don't just say there's a semicolon – explain what it does in this sentence.

b

two-part structure of second and third sentences	the idea of being in two minds ('ambivalent') is mirrored in the 'I enjoy … but fear'/ 'innovative drive … forms of domination' structure which balances good aspects with bad ones.

Exam tip: Remember to make sure you include a definition of 'ambivalent'.

Sentence Structure 4

An extract from an article in the Sunday Times *newspaper, in which Jeremy Clarkson writes about the way traditional television no longer appeals to children:*

> When I was eight, I watched Marine Boy because on a wet Thursday afternoon in October there was absolutely nothing else to do. Now, kids have got YouTube, Xbox, MSN, MySpace, text, e-mail, PSP, DVD and Sky+. All the world's ones and noughts have been harnessed for their edification and you're not going to drag them back to the box with a bunch of jolly-what-tally-ho Enid Blyton kids in big shorts getting into scrapes with smugglers. That was then, and it's as gone as the ruff and tuberculosis.

Q Show how the writer's sentence structure helps clarify the point he is making.

ANSWERS »

Possible answers:

list ('YouTube … Sky+')	makes clear the sheer number of alternatives to traditional TV
'When I was …'/ 'Now …'	contrasting openings of the first two sentences draw attention to the change over time
'That was then …'	brief, assertive final sentence sums up how far in the past the traditional seems.

Sentence Structure 5

An extract from an article in the London Review of Books *magazine, in which John Lanchester argues that most video games are not, as critics claim, 'escapist':*

> Most games, far from being pure entertainment, are work-like. They have a tightly designed structure in which the player has to earn points to win specific rewards, on the way to completing levels which earn him the right to play on other levels, earn more points to win other rewards, and so on, all of it repetitive, quantified and structured.
>
> The people who play them move from an education, much of it spent in front of a computer screen, full of competitive, repetitive, quantifiable, measured progress towards goals determined by others, to a work life, much of it spent in front of a computer screen, full of competitive, repetitive, quantifiable, measured progress towards goals determined by others, and for recreation sit in front of a computer screen and play games full of competitive, repetitive, quantifiable, measured progress towards goals determined by others. Most video games aren't nearly irresponsible enough.

Q How does the sentence structure of the second paragraph emphasise the point the writer is making about video games not being 'irresponsible enough'?

ANSWERS))

Key point

The writer's description of three elements in a gamer's life – education, work, recreation – is structured in exactly the same way and uses exactly the same words; this implies that they are all the same and that the 'recreational' element has none of the irresponsible behaviour normally associated with leisure activities, but is the same as work and school.

Secondary points

- the use of a list within each element suggests how much has to be done/that it is a chore
- the sound-effect gained by the repetition of 'competitive, repetitive' creates a machine-like monotony which emphasises how similar all the activities are.

Sentence Structure 6

An extract from an article in the Guardian *newspaper, in which the novelist Philip Pullman is critical of the way reading is taught in schools:*

> I recently read through the sections on reading in stages 1 to 3 of the national literacy strategy. I was very struck by something about the verbs. I wrote them all down. They included "reinforce", "predict", "check", "discuss", "identify", "categorise", "evaluate", "distinguish", "summarise", "infer", "analyse", "locate" ... and so on: 71 different verbs for the activities that come under the heading of "reading". And the word "enjoy" didn't appear once.

Q Show how the writer's sentence structure adds impact to the point he is making.

ANSWERS ▶▶

Possible answers:

three simple sentences at the start	suggests he is being very straightforward, calm, leading gently into the strong condemnation which is about to come
list of verbs quoted	12 items meticulously quoted to make clear just how huge the list of activities is
'… and so on'	as if he has made the point but wants to remind us that the list goes on and on
colon	introduces summary of what has gone before, including the startling total of 71 different verbs
final sentence	short, unadorned statement of the chilling absence of what (to the writer) is the idea that really matters.

Sentence Structure 7

An extract from an article in the Scotsman *newspaper, in which Larry Kane, 25 years after the shooting of John Lennon, attempts to sum up the musician's life:*

> John Lennon was a man of peace who could be at war with himself. He was a strong-willed man who became weak from abused substances. He was a rich man who felt for the poor. He made love to many women, but he loved only three. His life was constantly reinvented, his genius sometimes sapped by his own demons. In life, he was a creator and inventor. In death, he became an icon. He was a man who carried one single passport, but was always, without doubt, in life and death, a citizen of the world.

Q Show how the sentence structure of this paragraph conveys the writer's personal opinion of John Lennon.

ANSWERS 》》

Possible answers:

series of opposites	'peace … war'; 'strong-willed … weak'; 'rich … poor'; 'many … only three' – emphasise the writer's view that Lennon was riddled with contradictions, was uncertain of his own self
list-like structure ('He was … He was …')	emphasises how many aspects of his character displayed this duality
contrast of 'constantly … sometimes'	suggests the good things ('reinvented') were greater, more powerful than the bad ('sapped by … demons')
'In life, he … In death, he …'	creates focus on the difference between his energy when alive and the fixed, emblematic status in which he is now held
final sentence	returns to the 'He was …' plus contradiction ('single passport'/'citizen of the world') structure as if rounding off the description; enhanced by bringing the 'life and death' idea from the previous sentences, and by climaxing on the idea of 'citizen of the world'.

Sentence Structure 8

An extract from an article in the National Geographic *magazine, in which Brook Larmer discusses the world's enduring obsession with gold:*

Gold is not vital to human existence; it has, in fact, relatively few practical uses. Yet its chief virtues – its unusual density and malleability along with its imperishable shine – have made it one of the world's most coveted commodities, a transcendent symbol of beauty, wealth, and immortality. From pharaohs (who insisted on being buried in what they called the "flesh of the gods") to the forty-niners (whose mad rush for the mother lode built the American West) to the financiers (who, following Sir Isaac Newton's advice, made it the bedrock of the global economy): nearly every society through the ages has invested gold with an almost mythological power.

Q   Show how the writer's sentence structure clarifies what he is saying about the attraction of gold. Refer in detail to the final sentence and to at least one feature of sentence structure elsewhere in the paragraph.

ANSWERS ▶▶

Possible answers:

semicolon	allows balance between "vital to human existence" and "few practical uses" to point out the contradiction between perception and reality
parenthetical 'in fact'	emphasises the contradiction
parenthetical 'its unusual … shine'	inserts clear explanation of the 'virtues'
list: 'beauty, wealth and immortality'	points out the range of attractions
structure of final sentence	<ul><li>overall periodic structure: main idea of enduring and widespread obsession delayed until end</li><li>'From … to … to' builds up to climactic statement about 'mythological power'</li><li>within the build up the key elements are alliterative ('pharaohs … forty-niners … financier') adding a poetic resonance to the elements</li><li>series of bracketed parentheses adding additional information explaining a key feature of each group's interest in gold</li><li>colon introduces climax/summation of the general obsession with gold.</li></ul>

Sentence Structure 9

An extract from an article in the Independent *newspaper, in which Jenny McCartney begins a discussion of violence in movies with a reference to the new Batman film:*

> If I were 10 years old, would I be badgering my parents to take me to see the new Batman film, *The Dark Knight*? You bet I would. It's the latest and biggest release in the superhero genre, which children instantly understand as a direct appeal to their special interests.
>
> If I were the parent who relented and took a 10-year-old to see *The Dark Knight*, would I be sorry? You bet I would. It's different from other superhero films, surprising even me – after years spent as a film critic – with its sustained level of intensely sadistic brutality.

Q Show how the structure of these paragraphs adds impact to what the writer is saying.

ANSWERS ▶▶

Both paragraphs are carefully structured in a very similar way, for example:

- they start with an 'If I were … would I be' question
- both questions are about going to see the same film
- both questions are answered identically: 'You bet I would'
- the third sentence begins 'It's …' and tells us about the appeal/non-appeal of the film.

The effect is to highlight powerfully the difference between the expectation (that the film will conform to the superhero genre and will appeal to children) and the reality (that even a seasoned film critic is shocked at the violence in it).

***Exam* tip:** Note that this question refers not to 'sentence structure' but to 'structure'. They're similar, of course, but subtly different. 'Structure' on its own asks you to take an overview of the paragraphs, rather than get bogged down in small details. For example, the parenthetical '– after years spent as a film critic –' in the second paragraph is a feature of sentence structure but is not relevant to the overall structure of the paragraphs.

Sentence Structure 10

An extract from an article in The Times *newspaper, in which Janice Turner compares her reaction to a power cut with her son's reaction:*

> We had a power cut on Tuesday evening. I sat in the dark, oddly relaxed. No e-mail. No telly. Not enough torchlight to read by.
>
> Meanwhile, my younger son thrashed from room to room, between Wii console, computer and TV, fretting that the shows he had Sky-plussed wouldn't record, scrabbling to see how much charge was left in his brother's laptop so that he might, at very least, watch a movie.
>
> When I laughed at his techno-junkie despair he exclaimed in white-hot fury: "It's all right for you. To me it's ... it's like living in poverty."

Q Show how sentence structure helps to emphasise the contrast in reactions between the writer and her son.

ANSWERS ▶▶

Writer/mother

series of short/minor sentences	creates calm, unemotional mood, simply accepts the situation.

Son

long, detailed sentence	creates breathless, hectic mood as if frantically rushing around
'To me it's ... it's like living in poverty'	structure suggests boy is so worked up he can't get the words out.

General point

positioning of 'Meanwhile'	implies some contrast is going to emerge with the mother's reaction in the previous paragraph.

***Exam* tip:** When the writer/mother is being described, there is a noticeable repetition of the word 'no', but it would be very difficult to relate this to her state of mind.

Writer's Language 1

An extract from an article in the Scotland on Sunday *newspaper, in which Joanna Blythman, writing about the announcement that two pandas are coming to Edinburgh Zoo, wonders if zoos are about education or entertainment:*

> But then entertainment is what zoos are all about. The main thing that distinguishes them from the discredited circuses of yesteryear is their spurious educational credentials. But what does a child really learn from watching a wretched polar bear sitting disconsolately on some concrete rock? What ecological awareness is gleaned from the looking into an enclosure, watching a listless tiger pacing up and down with frustrated, stereotypic movements? Don't ask me. I refused to take my children to a zoo because I find them so depressing. But they went with school anyway, and found them … depressing.

Q Show how the writer's use of language makes clear her disapproval of zoos. Refer in your answer to word choice and sentence structure.

Note: There is no specific mark allocation in this Writer's Language section – see paragraph two of the Introduction, page 4.

ANSWERS ▶▶

Word Choice

Possible answers:

spurious	suggests claims to educational value are bogus, misleading
wretched	suggests animal is miserable, ill-treated
disconsolately	suggests animal is sad, without companionship
concrete rock	suggests zoo environment is harsh, unnatural
listless	suggests animal is lethargic, lacking spirit
frustrated	suggests animal is irritated, suffering because of confined environment
stereotypic	suggests animal is limited to the predictable, forced to conform.

Sentence Structure

Possible answers:

(rhetorical) questions	hectoring tone, demanding the answer 'None' as if bullying the reader
'Don't ask me.'	blunt, dismissive short sentence as if not prepared to engage in debate
'and found them … depressing'	deliberately delaying final word teases the reader before revealing the 'surprise', which is in fact predictable
repetition of 'depressing'	to emphasise just how disheartening zoos are, not just to her but to her children.

Writer's Language 2

An extract from an article in the Herald *newspaper, in which Ian Bell defends JK Rowling, author of the Harry Potter books, against criticism that she is too concerned with money:*

> JK Rowling will never win the Nobel prize for Literature. On any technical level, her writing is not brilliant. But what use is brilliant writing if – the usual result – it isn't read? Fiction isn't supposed to be grand opera. It has only recently pretended to be an art.
>
> Dickens knew all about these things. He offended his betters by making absurd amounts of money. He flogged cheap editions on railway platforms. They called him a hack, and denounced "Dickensian" as a marketing game. He didn't deny a word of it. His only answer was that he was a writer, first and last: his job was to make people read.
>
> Rowling's glory is that she caused an epidemic of childhood reading in a digital world.

Q Show how the writer's use of language highlights the points he is making in this extract. Refer to at least one appropriate language feature in each paragraph.

ANSWERS ▶▶

Possible answers:

rhetorical question: 'But what use is …'	invites reader to agree with point that 'art' in fiction is pointless if hardly anyone reads it
parenthesis: '– the usual result –'	underlines point that arty books aren't widely read by adding in that this is in fact what usually happens
'absurd amounts of money'	emphasises just how enormous his earnings were and how little his 'betters' were able to understand it
'flogged'	use of colloquialism tends to suggest how little Dickens cared for 'proper' behaviour
'hack'	demeaning term suggests how strongly he was despised
'glory'	suggests magnificence, splendour, making clear his admiration for her achievements
imagery of 'epidemic'	just as an epidemic spreads quickly and affects large numbers of people, so Rowling caused a huge upsurge in the numbers of children reading books (despite the challenge from digital media).

***Exam* tip:** Remember that in questions about 'the writer's use of language' you aren't always given instructions or suggestions about which features to refer to. If you're not, think about all the usual possibilities: word choice, sentence structure, imagery, tone, sound, contrast – and choose ones you can answer easily. If the question has been left open it means there will always be plenty to choose from.

Writer's Language 3

An extract from an article in the Observer *newspaper, in which Barbara Ellen challenges a claim that middle-class children are likely to be more 'academically gifted' because of their parents' genes:*

Behind most "academically outstanding" middle-class children, there are likely to be frazzled, micromanaging parents, working very hard to ensure their child gets ahead. I know this, because I've been there and I know many who've been much further. There is a dark, complicated dance that goes on behind closed doors between worried parent and exam-aged child: fretting, planning, chivvying, coaxing, bribing, begging, not to mention the threats and groundings when they don't play ball.

· For their sins, "maxi-strength" parents know this. Get a glass of wine down them and the truth pours out. Few of them would pretend that their little darlings did it all alone. Or deny the power of the £50-per-A bribe (sorry, deal) they made with them at the last minute. They know to what extent they've been the thrashing webbed feet beneath the gliding swan of their child's academic success.

Q Show how the writer's use of language conveys the extent to which middle-class parents are involved in their children's academic success. Refer to a range of appropriate language features in your answer.

ANSWERS ▶▶

Possible answers:

inverted commas at 'academically gifted'	makes it clear that their academic qualities are questionable and implies there is some other reason for their success
'frazzled'	suggests the parents will work to the point of desperation and near-exhaustion to help their children
'micromanaging'	suggests parents are involved in controlling every little aspect of the child's life, possibly suggests bringing a business model to it
'dark, complicated dance'	imagery suggests some kind of ritualistic pattern, agreed steps in which success depends on the two partners figuring out how to work together
list of activities in the 'dance'	suggests how extensive/complex it is; also preponderance of present participles suggest much activity
use of 'maxi-strength'	humorous comparison to some kind of industrial cleaner, etc. suggests these are the parents who consciously put in as much effort as possible
'bribe (sorry deal)'	open admission that the children are offered financial inducements despite the tongue-in-cheek 'correction' in parenthesis
'the thrashing webbed feet beneath the gliding swan'	just as a swan is said to look calm and elegant on the surface despite frantic movements below, so the apparent ease of the child's achievement is really thanks to the efforts of the parent.

Writer's Language 4

An extract from a blog on the website of the Herald *newspaper on 10 August 2011, in which Kate Higgins reflects on the riots and looting in London and other cities:*

> We think we can treat young people with contempt, demand respect when it has not been earned, consign them to a lifetime of poverty, disregard their need for education and nurture, cut their services first and hardest, and cast them on to the scrapheap of life in order to preserve our own cosy lifestyles.
>
> Consequently, young people are rioting not just because they can, but because it is all they can do. Hope is an unfamiliar companion, the idea of generational justice is laughable and nihilism is the order of the day. They have no fear because they have no future.

Q Show how the writer's use of language in these paragraphs makes clear her sympathy with the young people she is describing. Refer to sentence structure, word choice and imagery in your answer.

ANSWERS ⟩⟩

Possible answers:

list: 'treat ... with contempt', 'demand', 'consign', 'cut', 'cast'	emphasises the large number of negative ways in which adults treat young people
word choice within the list	all suggest lack of care/consideration, all suggest dismissive treatment, idea of throwing them aside
'scrapheap'	suggests they are treated as rejects, as not worthy of attention, as just so much garbage
'own cosy lifestyles'	highlights the contrast with adults' smug contentment
structure of 'not just ... but'	emphasises the hopelessness of their position by adding the idea that they have no alternative
'Hope is an unfamiliar companion.'	personification of 'hope' as someone they rarely meet or get to know emphasises the bleakness of their position
'laughable'	conveys their view of justice as something unattainable and ridiculous
'nihilism'	suggests the total rejection of hope, the belief that there are no principles worth believing in, the desire to overthrow existing institutions
structure of final sentence	careful balancing of 'no fear' and 'no future' around 'because' makes clear she thinks there is a simple, very bleak explanation – made more powerful by the alliteration ('fear/future') almost as if it's an undeniably true statement.

Writer's Language 5

An extract from an article in the Independent *newspaper, in which Tom Utley describes his reaction to seeing the world-famous painting* Mona Lisa:

> When I finally saw the *Mona Lisa*, after my 50 years on this Earth, I found it a terrible disappointment. I don't know quite what I was expecting. I suppose that I was hoping at least for some glimmer of understanding of why this was the most talked-about painting in the world – at best, for a rush of joy at the sheer beauty of this, the real thing.
>
> What I got instead was, well, the *Mona Lisa* – looking exactly as she does on a trillion coffee mugs, posters and tea-towels the world over.
>
> My fellow tourists and I were not really at the Louvre in quest of aesthetic pleasure. We were there just to tick the box marked "*Mona Lisa*". We traipse around galleries because we know that this is a civilised thing to do. We certainly try to enjoy what we see, and of course some paintings strike us as quite pleasing. But not as pleasing as all that.

Q Show how the writer's use of language in the second and third paragraphs conveys his sense of disappointment at visiting art galleries in general and seeing the *Mona Lisa* in particular. Refer to at least two different language features in your answer.

ANSWERS ▶▶

Possible answers:

'was, well, the *Mona Lisa*'	stumbling, interrupted utterance, as if he can't find words to express it properly, to convey the sense of emptiness, of let down, almost of incredulity
use of dash	to introduce expansion of the let down as if to say 'and what's worse'
list 'a trillion … towels'	the list of banal objects emphasises the sense of disappointment and shows how many such objects exist
exaggeration of 'trillion'	makes the ordinariness sound even worse
'tick the box'	suggests something routine, done as a chore, easily forgotten
'traipse'	suggests reluctant, plodding dutifully, absence of any pleasure
'But not as pleasing as that.'	short sentence gives sense of definite rejection (subverts the preceding idea of 'quite pleasing').

Writer's Language 6

An extract from an article in The Times *newspaper, in which Ben Macintyre reveals his appreciation of the British Museum in London:*

> The British Museum is the greatest universal museum in the world. On my first visit there, as a teenager, I remember feeling physically overwhelmed by the sheer scale and variety of the artefacts, art and ideas on display: Mesopotamian relics, Roman statuary, pharaonic carvings, Viking burial treasures.
>
> I wandered, blinking, from room to room. The museum was not trying to tell me something; it seemed to be offering to tell me everything.

Q Show how the writer's use of language conveys how deeply he was affected by his first visit to the museum. Refer to at least two appropriate language features in your answer.

ANSWERS ⟩⟩

Possible answers:

'greatest'	superlative adjective makes clear that he thinks it is without parallel
'physically overwhelmed'	conveys the idea that he reacted with something like dizziness, as if his senses were being assaulted, swamped
'sheer scale'	suggests the enormity of the range of exhibits, almost too big to comprehend
'artefacts, art and ideas'	list of the many types of exhibit emphasises the range of things on show
colon	introduces expansion of statement about 'scale and variety'
list ('Mesopotamian … treasures')	emphasises the number and historical/geographical diversity of the artefacts
'blinking'	suggests near-disbelief at what he was seeing, as if he had to keep opening and closing his eyes to reassure himself it was true
structure of 'I wandered, blinking, from room to room.'	staccato structure suggests he is slightly dazed, uncertain of his bearings
structure of final sentence	carefully balanced ('not trying/offering', 'tell me something/tell me everything') for effect, builds up to awestruck idea of being informed about everything in the world
personification of museum	suggests it is like some benign, omniscient being with the power to bestow universal knowledge and understanding.

Writer's Language 7

An extract from an article in the Herald *newspaper, in which Ron Ferguson argues against the claim that Britain is a 'Christian nation':*

The notion of a "Christian nation" is a myth. When, precisely, was England, or Scotland, a Christian nation? In the Middle Ages, for instance, Christianity was clearly the dominant thought form – in lip-service if not always in personal belief – but the idea that the punters all signed up to all the doctrines of orthodox faith is without credible evidence. It's a romantic and theologically incoherent construct.

Even in Victorian Britain, the gin palaces wreaked as much social havoc as binge-drinking today. Religion had an important part to play in the lives of individuals who sought to break the chains of addiction and, indeed, created movements that improved the lives of many people, but the narrative of a Christian consensus in a "Christian nation" leading to widespread good behaviour is hokum.

Q Show how the writer's use of language makes clear his rejection of the idea that Britain is a 'Christian nation'. Refer to sentence structure, word choice and tone in your answer.

ANSWERS >>

Possible answers:

'notion'	suggests something rather fanciful, certainly not factual and provable
use of inverted commas	cast doubts on the authenticity of the term 'Christian nation', as if writer is deliberately distancing himself from it
'myth'	suggests he sees it as something without any foundation, as a story that has grown over time, might be appealing but has no basis
'When, precisely, …'	rather argumentative tone created by the insertion of 'precisely', as if challenging the reader
parenthetical '– in lip-service if not always in personal belief –'	deliberately undercuts the concession that Christianity was the dominant way of thinking by suggestion that many people were not being serious and were only doing it to keep up appearances ('lip-service')
'punters'	use of slang term implies lack of respect for the argument he is negating
'romantic'	suggests it is starry-eyed, wishful thinking
'incoherent'	suggests it lacks any logical thinking, is confused, rambling
'construct'	suggests it's made up, purely theoretical, possibly intended to deceive
structure of last sentence	starts with admission that religion/Christianity did have positive features; then 'but' rejects the idea that proves universality
'hokum'	suggests absolute nonsense, some sort of cheap stage trick.

Writer's Language 8

An extract from an article in the Herald *newspaper, in which the writer argues that horse racing is cruel and should be banned:*

> At weekends in Spain, thousands of people watch animals being used for sport; they watch them abused, they watch them killed. We think: how foreign, how cruel, but then we do the same thing here. At weekends in Britain, thousands of people watch horses being used for sport, they watch them being abused and they watch them killed.
>
> If you think there is no abuse, what is whipping? The British gentleman used to be allowed to whip his wife, his servant, his child, his dog (damn it, it was good for them) but now the whip is allowed only on the racecourse. As for killing, every year, around 100 horses die on the racecourse, in public, in the open. People stand and watch legs snap, necks shatter, backs break; they watch horses flail and squirm in agony; they watch them die.

Q Show how the writer's use of language makes clear her disapproval of horse racing. Refer to at least two appropriate language features in your answer.

ANSWERS ▶▶

Possible answers:

parallel structure in first paragraph	'At weekends … thousands of people … used for sport … watch them abused … watched them killed' – drives home that Britain is similar to Spain, which is criticised for cruelty to animals
repetition of key words: 'used … abused … killed'	shows her disapproval by using powerfully emotive words to describes the way the animals are treated
'If you think … what is whipping?'	aggressive, challenging tone; direct address to 'you' and a question demanding an answer
'The British gentleman … for them)'	sarcastically describes long-gone practices and the ridiculous, out of date attitudes it involved to highlight the absurdity of its still being allowed on the racecourse
'on the racecourse, in public, in the open'	repetitive structure, rather hectoring tone, angrily emphasising how visible the practice is
'stand and watch'	suggests their passivity and implies her disapproval of this
'snap, shatter, break'	highly emotive words, onomatopoeic effect to bring home the horror
'flail and squirm'	conveys powerfully the horses' uncontrolled movements, their disorientation and pain
repetition of 'watch'	emphasises the passive acceptance of the spectators.

Writer's Language 9

An extract from an article in The Times *newspaper, in which Ben Macintyre argues that the Internet is changing the way we read:*

> Click, tweet, skim, blog, browse, scan, text: the jargon of the digital age describes how we now read. The information we consume online comes ever faster, punchier and more fleetingly. Our attention rests only briefly on the Internet page before moving on to the next electronic canapé. Hectored and heckled by the next blog alert or text message, we are too bombarded by snippets of information to focus on anything for very long. The Internet has evolved a new species of magpie reader, gathering bright little buttons of knowledge, before hopping on to the next shiny thing.

Q Show how the writer's use of language conveys his attitude to:

a the experience of reading on the Internet.
b the nature of the information we read on the Internet.

ANSWERS ▶▶

Possible answers:

All could reasonably be applied to **a** or **b**:

list ('Click, tweet …')	list to emphasise the range of different activities
the string of monosyllabic words	makes the experience sound fast, punchy, almost aggressive
'jargon'	pejorative term suggesting designed to confuse
'(more) fleetingly'	suggests experience is rapid, ephemeral
imagery of 'canapé'	just as a canapé is a small, insubstantial type of food, so the Internet provides bite-size, easy but lightweight information
'hectored'	suggests aggressive, demanding attention
'heckled'	suggests rude, interrupting, no peace to decide for yourself
'bombarded'	suggests a sustained attack
'snippets'	suggests scraps, bits and pieces, lack of development or coherence
imagery of 'magpie'	just as a magpie randomly collects odds and ends, so the experience for the Internet reader lacks coherence or pattern
'bright'/'shiny'	suggest superficial attractiveness
'(little) buttons'	suggests the information is trivial
'hopping'	suggests quick, light, carefree movement, as if all of no importance.

Writer's Language 10

An extract from an article in The Times *newspaper, in which Libby Purves discusses faults in the way news is reported:*

> These days, "news" is a jabber, a fluster, a blizzard of bloggery. We tolerate correspondents who blur news and commentary without even recognising it. We watch the mission to explain turning into a licence to witter. We are aware, as broadband spreads across the world, that the most thoughtful and well-researched article posted online will instantly grow a long tail of comments, many of them mad or irrelevant. We accept that "citizen journalists" with photo-phones and unchecked facts are now ordained as democratising saviours, liberating society from the tyranny of competence and expertise. We are treated nightly to speculation and opinion stirred like luscious raisins into the thin gruel of fact.

Q Show how the writer's use of language in these paragraphs conveys her dissatisfaction with the way news is presented. Refer to a range of appropriate language features in your answer.

ANSWERS))

Possible answers:

'jabber'	suggests incoherent, babbling, meaningless
'fluster'	suggests confused, muddled
'blizzard of bloggery'	image of 'blizzard' compares reporting to a powerful snowstorm which blanks out vision, i.e. prevents understanding and clarity
	alliteration has rather harsh, condemnatory sound (or is deliberately comic)
	invented word 'bloggery' is dismissively comic, contemptuous
'blur (news and commentary)'	suggests confusion, lack of ability to tell the difference, creation of vagueness
'(without) even (recognising)'	emphasises their incompetence, their lack of ability to tell the difference.

the contrast between 'mission to explain' (sounds noble and valuable) and 'licence to witter' (as if granted permission to talk nonsense) emphasises the difference

irony in 'ordained as democratising saviours liberating' – using religious terminology as if they were granted saint-like powers to bring wisdom to the world

paradox of 'the tyranny of competence and expertise' – desirable qualities are now seen as getting in the way of good reporting

complex image of 'stirred like luscious raisins into the thin gruel of fact' suggesting that the speculation is simply an attempt to add substance to the limited facts available, to dress up a meagre dish ('thin gruel') with appealing, but tiny ('luscious raisins') extras.

Tone 1

An extract from an article in the Independent *newspaper, in which Terence Blacker explains how some land developers will do well from an announcement in the Budget:*

> A few years ago, spivs working in the development sector hit on a cracking new wheeze. They bought fields outside towns and villages where plans to develop had been denied by the local council. Then they sold small housing plots, assuring would-be buyers that, sooner or later, planning restrictions would be relaxed, earning the investor a fat profit. It was certainly a nice little earner for the developer. Councils responded to these schemes with outrage, but buyers poured in.
>
> Now, thanks to the Government, the land-sharks who worked the deal will soon be in the money.

Q Show how the writer creates a tone of contempt for the developers.

Note: There is no specific mark allocation in this Tone section – see paragraph two of the Introduction, page 4.

ANSWERS

Possible answers:

A general comment could be made about how the extensive use of slang expressions ('spivs … cracking new wheeze … fat profit … nice little earner … land-sharks … in the money') makes the developers sound cheap, coarse, unreliable, etc.

Or individual word/expressions could be explored to arrive at the same conclusion, for example:

'spivs'	shady, criminal characters
'wheeze'	as if it's all a joke, not a serious business proposition
'fat profit'	sounds greedy, grotesque
'nice little earner'	sounds like the language of a petty criminal
'land-sharks'	makes them sound predatory, ruthless
'in the money'	sounds smug, self-interested.

***Exam* tip:** Questions on tone are always difficult. It's often easy to sense how the tone is being created, but usually difficult to explain how it's being done. Good advice is to imagine it being read aloud and trying to 'hear' how particular words or structures have an effect.

Tone 2

An extract from an article in The Times *newspaper, in which Richard Morrison is critical of what schools do to young people:*

> At the same time the fetish with league tables has forced teachers to turn schools into fact-cramming, rote-learning factories in which narrowly focused lessons are reinforced by stacks of homework. Our education system is now as blinkered, as grindingly utilitarian, as in the era mocked by Dickens in *Hard Times*. Is it any wonder that so many school-leavers have no pastimes except shopping, watching telly and binge-drinking?

Q Show how the writer's angry tone is conveyed.

ANSWERS ▶▶

Possible answers:

'fetish'	use of word usually associated with some sort of perverted obsession shows just how much contempt he has for the league tables
'fact-cramming, rote-learning'	two compound words which make the schools sound aggressive, relentless – the words are squeezed together in a way to suggest the grinding oppression involved
'factories'	comparing schools to factories shows he sees them as being designed simply to churn out 'product', soulless, mechanical, utilitarian
'blinkered … grindingly utilitarian'	suggesting they have no vision, are simply there to do a job and do it oppressively
reference to Dickens	scathing reminder that over 150 years ago this approach to education was being seen as worthy of mockery
final sentence	rhetorical question demanding agreement with his angry summation of the effect on school-leavers almost despairing tone of 'Is it any wonder …' deliberately chooses 'uncultured' activities as examples of what they're reduced to, with the 'binge drinking' almost symbolic of teenage irresponsibility.

Tone 3

An extract from an article in The Times *newspaper, in which Rachel Sylvester is unimpressed that MPs have started using Twitter:*

> Hey there! The Prime Minister is using Twitter. It's true. You can, on the Downing Street website, read a blow-by-blow account of the Prime Minister's day. If that thought isn't terrifying enough, dozens of other politicians have also signed up to the social networking site that lets users answer (in 140 letters or fewer) the question: "What are you doing now?"
>
> Middle-aged MPs hope they will look youthful and "in touch" if they use the latest web tool. But there is a slight Dad-on-the-dancefloor feel to some of their attempts. The content is all too often less twitter than witter. Is the reputation of politics really enhanced by the revelation that the Schools Minister, is "snowed under with paperwork" or that the Opposition housing spokesman is "contemplating taking my eldest son to play football in the rain" or that a nondescript MP "can't find the TV remote control"?

Q Show how the writer creates a tone that makes fun of the idea of politicians using Twitter.

ANSWERS ▶▶

Possible answers:

Use of 'Hey there!' at start – imitates and mocks the bright, breezy, informal style of Twitter which seems out of place when talking about the Prime Minister.

'If that thought isn't terrifying enough …' – exaggeration (it's hardly 'terrifying') to show how ridiculous she thinks it is.

'Dad-on-the-dancefloor' – idea of someone who looks out of place, trying to be something he's not, trying to be trendy, embarrassing, etc; makes the politicians sound very silly.

'less twitter than witter' – wordplay to suggest the politicians are 'wittering on'.

The examples of politicians' Twitter messages are uniformly banal, showing how absurd it is for people involved in running the country to be indulging in such nonsense.

Tone 4

An extract from an article in the National Geographic *magazine, in which Joel Achenbach describes CERN's Large Hadron Collider:*

> If you were to dig a hole 300 feet straight down from the centre of the charming French village of Crozet, you'd pop into a setting that calls to mind the subterranean lair of one of those James Bond villains. A garishly lit tunnel ten feet in diameter curves away into the distance, interrupted every few miles by lofty chambers crammed with heavy steel structures, cables, pipes, wires, magnets, tubes, shafts, catwalks, and enigmatic gizmos.
>
> This technological netherworld is one very big scientific instrument, a particle accelerator – an atomic peashooter more powerful than any ever built. It's called the Large Hadron Collider, and its purpose is simple but ambitious: to crack the code of the physical world; to figure out what the universe is made of; in other words, to get to the very bottom of things.

Q Show how the writer, although describing a complex scientific process, uses a light-hearted tone.

ANSWERS))

Possible answers:

'pop into'	very colloquial term, nothing threatening
'… lair of one of those James Bond villains'	uses reference to well-known stereotype locations, familiar from films, of gigantic caves filled with outlandish machinery, a setting which has become almost a parody of itself
'gizmos'	slang term for technological device, suggests writer is not by any means a specialist, shares reader's possible ignorance
'atomic peashooter'	humorously reduces complex apparatus to level of a very basic childhood toy
'crack the code'/ 'get to the very bottom of things'	rather informal descriptions of the hugely complex goal (understand what the universe is made of).

Exam tip: Don't just identify the obviously light-hearted words/phrases: there needs to be some explanation of their effect, of what makes them sound light-hearted.

Tone 5

An extract from an article in the Herald *newspaper, in which Julian Baggini takes issue with the claim that the promotion of elite sports such as the Olympics is good for the health and well-being of the nation:*

> If you want to promote health and fitness, you're almost certainly better off channelling funds directly to those whom you'd like to see get off their backsides, rather than to those who are already hardly ever on them. People say our Olympians inspire people to get out and do it themselves, but most sporting spectacles inspire people to do no more than order a pizza and slump in front of the telly. To mix my metaphors, for the trickle-down effect argument to hold any water, you'd need some evidence that sporting performance at the elite level has some relation to wider sporting participation. But evidence for this is thin on the ground.

Q Show how the writer's dismissive tone about the claim is made clear.

ANSWERS ▶▶

Possible answers:

'get off their backsides'	a colloquial, rather coarse, rude description of the inactive among the population, suggesting he is not taking the idea very seriously
'hardly ever on them'	a rather humorous description of the athletes, reducing their sporting prowess to them simply not being on their 'backsides'
'order a pizza'	stereotypical view of the self-indulgent, non-sporty, consumer of junk food
'slump'	suggests they are lazy, sprawling (polar opposite of athletic grace)
'telly'	slovenliness extends even to referring to television by slang name
'mix my metaphors'	implies perhaps that he is not too bothered with 'proper' expression, that the claim is not worthy of this
'thin on the ground'	sounds very much like a euphemism for 'non-existent', he is being a little tongue-in-cheek.

Tone 6

An extract from an article in The Times *newspaper, in which Carol Midgley writes about 'The Myths of Cohabitation':*

A university study has found that women agree to live with a partner because they see it as a step towards marriage, while men agree because they think they'll get more sex. Pause briefly to digest this stunning news. What would we do without universities, eh?

What would have been more useful was a study into who turns out to be right. Do most women get a ring on their finger and most men unlimited legover after moving in together? Because scientific research from the University of Pub Conversations suggests both should prepare for disappointment. Especially the men.

Q Show how the writer's mocking tone is created in these paragraphs.

ANSWERS ▶▶

Possible answers:

'Pause briefly …'	sounding like a tour guide, or lecturer, as if it's a serious subject, when in fact she thinks it's daft
'stunning news'	clearly ironic – she thinks it's quite the opposite
'What would we do without universities, eh?'	sounding superficially as if she thinks they're indispensable when she clearly means they're a waste of time; the 'eh' at the end sounds as if she is in awe of their achievements, but simply adds to the mockery
'ring on their finger … unlimited legover'	reduces the two topics to rather crude basics, suggesting strongly that she isn't taking things very seriously
'scientific research from the University of Pub Conversations'	humorous contradiction 'scientific research … Pub Conversations' as well as suggestion that such a University might actually exist shows she is being entirely tongue-in-cheek
'Especially the men.'	throwaway remark (from a female writer) mocking men for their lack of success in securing more sex.

Tone 7

An extract from an article in the Herald *newspaper, in which Andrew Mackie discusses plans to ban animals in circuses:*

> The book *Animal Liberation* by Professor Peter Singer, the Australian philosopher, popularised the idea of "speciesism". His conclusions, based on the proposition that the differences between human beings and other animals are merely those of degree, suggest that human rights should be extended to other species: farms, zoos, meat-eating and leather should be outlawed; and all aspects of animal husbandry abandoned; and the great apes should be represented at the United Nations. There would be no logical basis for distinguishing between the rights of a person and those of a shrimp. One suspects that this theory doesn't have widespread support.

Q Show how the writer creates a dismissive tone about Professor Singer's idea.

ANSWERS ▶▶

Possible answers:

use of inverted commas around 'speciesism' suggests a sort of distancing from the term, as if the author finds it mildly ridiculous, or is drawing attention to what a strange, outlandish word it is.

the very scientific phraseology of most of the second sentence ('proposition … merely those of degree … extended … species … aspects of animal husbandry') clashes violently with the bizarre concept of great apes being represented at the UN.

the absence of any explicit comment on the ape at the UN idea simply makes it sound all the more ridiculous.

the extreme example 'shrimp' (symbolic of very primitive life) as something equivalent to a person serves to make the idea sound silly.

the very formal and restrained 'One suspects … widespread support' is really a euphemism for 'Nearly everyone thinks he's mad'.

Tone 8

An extract from an article in the Herald *newspaper, in which Ron Ferguson takes issue with campaigners who are critical of the commercialisation of Christmas and want to 'put Christ back into Christmas':*

> My problem with the "putting Christ back into Christmas" stuff is that much of it is nostalgic and sentimental hokum played out against a background of the ringing of tills. Its relationship with the historical Jesus is very tenuous indeed. The idealised Italianate pictures of a blue-robed, cream-complexioned Madonna with her (non-crying, of course) child conceal the fact that the real Mary would have been a swarthy Jewish peasant girl. The song attributed to this young woman by the gospel writers is not one that would have brought a smile to the face of the Jerusalem Chamber of Commerce: it is a revolutionary hymn that predicts a new world order in which the mighty will be cast down from their thrones and the poor will be exalted. If Christ is put back into Christmas, will these uncomfortable words be relayed through the Christmas shopping malls? Er, no.

Q Explain how the writer's scornful tone is conveyed in this paragraph.

ANSWERS ▶▶

Possible answers:

the use of 'stuff' to describe the campaign reduces it to something vague and hardly worthy of consideration.

calling it 'nostalgic and sentimental' suggests it is over-romanticised, corny, unrealistic.

'hokum' suggests something nonsensical, even deceptive, designed simply to please.

'background of ringing tills' points contemptuously to the commercial motives behind it.

the parenthetical '(not crying, of course)' is mocking the unrealistic depiction of a baby.

the invention of a 'Jerusalem Chamber of Commerce' humorously reminds us of the threat to commercial interests.

the rhetorical question forcefully brings out the idea that the 'real' Jesus would be a threat to commercial interests.

the answer 'Er, no.' is meant to sound as if it is blindingly simple, as if the stupidest person would know the answer.

Tone 9

An extract from an article in the Observer *newspaper, in which Carol Sarler defends 'inter-country adoption' from poor countries to the West against criticism from both ends of the political spectrum:*

> The fears from the right stem from suspicions that this is just another route for foreigners to 'flood' into the country and be a 'drain' on resources. To that I say, such posturing is too monstrous to address.
>
> The objections from the liberal left are just as shocking. Pundit after pundit drones on about the perils of 'snatching' children from their 'culture'. To that I say, go and stand in the orphanages of the world's most dispossessed; look, sniff, smell and don't – don't you dare – tell me that, in this context, the word 'culture' is other than an obscenity.

Q Show how the writer's contemptuous tone is created in these paragraphs.

ANSWERS ▶▶

Possible answers:

use of inverted commas around 'flood' and 'drain'	as if quoting sarcastically the knee-jerk, essentially racist, emotional reaction of right-wingers to 'foreigners'
'posturing'	suggests they are blustering, pompous, putting on a pathetic act
'monstrous'	makes them sound non-human, outrageous, as if the idea is too grotesque to consider, or even comment on
'Pundit after pundit'	sneering description of them as self-appointed experts, and repetition of the word gives idea of an endless, boring line of them
'drones on'	makes them sound tiresome, whining at length, saying the same thing over and over again
use of inverted commas around 'snatching' and 'culture'	as if quoting sarcastically the outraged objections of the liberal left, their use of emotional words to distort the reality
(second) use of 'To that I say …'	as if pointing a finger angrily at both sides
'go and stand … look, sniff, smell'	imperatives as if losing patience, giving simple instructions on how they can learn something
'don't – don't you dare – tell me'	really worked up now, challenging them not even to think about not agreeing with her, shows real contempt that they might even think of it
'obscenity'	final word emphasises just how disgusting, offensive she finds their claim.

Tone 10

An extract from an article in The Times *newspaper, in which Daniel Finkelstein gives his views on a report called* The Good Childhood Inquiry:

> Yesterday, with great fanfare, the results of *The Good Childhood Inquiry* were published. You probably read all about it. But let's just say, for a moment, that you didn't. I will provide a brutal summary. All part of the service.
>
> The inquiry concluded that children in Britain are unhappy. This is largely caused by the behaviour of their parents, especially working women. And this damaging behaviour results from the social evil of excessive individualism. There were a couple of hundred more pages, but that just about does it.
>
> Here is an equally brutal summary of my response. Children in this country are not unhappy. The inquiry presents no convincing evidence at all that children are being damaged by the behaviour of their parents or by women working. There is no reason to believe that our individualism is excessive or a social evil.
>
> Apart from that, I thought the report was terrific.

 Q   Show how the writer varies the tone in these paragraphs in order to convey his opinion of the report.

ANSWERS 》

Possible answers:

first paragraph	light-hearted tone throughout, created by: • 'fanfare' suggesting hyped-up importance of the report • chatty tone of 'you probably' and 'let's just say' • mock humility of 'All part of the service'
second paragraph	apparently serious tone until final sentence which undercuts this with a throwaway dismissal of 'a couple of hundred more pages'
third paragraph	serious, dogmatic tone throughout
fourth paragraph	deeply ironic tone – having dismissed the report in a couple of sentences, he claims, tongue-in-cheek, that the report is 'terrific', implying that it is anything but
overall effect	is to mock the report, by reducing its findings to a couple of sentences and then rejecting them utterly – followed by an improbable claim that 'Apart from that' (i.e., that the whole report is wrong) the report is 'terrific'.